TEACHERS LEARNING IN COMMUNITY

SUNY series, Restructuring and School Change
H. Dickson Corbett and Betty Lou Whitford, editors

TEACHERS LEARNING IN COMMUNITY

໑ • ໑

Realities and Possibilities

Edited by
Betty Lou Whitford
and
Diane R. Wood

Published by State University of New York Press, Albany

© 2010 State University of New York

For information, contact State University of New York Press, Albany, NY
www.sunypress.edu

Production by Diane Ganeles
Marketing by Michael Campochiaro

Library of Congress Cataloging-in-Publication Data
Teachers learning in community : realities and possibilities / edited by
Betty Lou Whitford and Diane R. Wood.
    p. cm. — (SUNY series, restructuring and school change)
Includes bibliographical references and indexes.
ISBN 978-1-4384-3061-4 (hardcover : alk. paper)
ISBN 978-1-4384-3060-7 (pbk. : alk. paper)
1. Professional learning communities—United States.
2. Teachers—In-service training—United States. I. Whitford, Betty Lou.
II. Wood, Diane R., 1946-
LB1731.T4199 2010
370.71'55—dc22
                                                                          2009023133

10 9 8 7 6 5 4 3 2 1

CONTENTS

ACKNOWLEDGMENTS

BETTY LOU WHITFORD AND DIANE R. WOOD

As with all long-term field studies, many people have been involved and made significant contributions to the research we conducted and the understandings we developed. Topping our list are the many teachers and administrators in seven school districts in five states who generously shared their time and insights with us. As we fanned out into their offices, schools, and classrooms, they graciously put aside pressing demands to answer questions and explain their perspectives. Many allowed us to watch them at work, and it is the work that they do that provided the core inspiration for this book. While not named to protect confidentiality agreements, they know who they are, and we extend each one our heartfelt thanks.

As explained in chapter 2, the research project was initially based at Teachers College, Columbia University, where Betty Lou Whitford, then director of the National Center for Restructuring Education, Schools, and Teaching (NCREST), served as principal investigator. Linda Darling-Hammond, Carla Asher, and Fred Frelow of the National Commission on Teaching and America's Future (NCTAF), also then based at Teachers College, contributed to the conceptualization of the research proposal. Heidi Fisher served as project manager, and research assistants included Ji-Sung Chong, Lindsay Stanley, and Christine Clayton.

In 2002, the project moved to the University of Southern Maine (USM) when Whitford became dean of the College of Education and Human Development. At USM, Debra R. Smith served as project manager and later as principal investigator of the research in New Jersey. Alison Moser, Chris Backiel, Ken Bedder, Laura O'Neill, and Robin Day contributed to project administration and data analysis. Lanna

Maheux-Quinn helped with transcription, and Judy Letarte and Kim Warren pitched in on short notice to solve some technological glitches encountered in preparing to submit the book manuscript to State University of New York (SUNY) Press. We are also grateful to Karen Fox whose keen eye helped immensely with copy editing in the final stages of manuscript preparation.

Though his name does not appear on any of the chapters, Edu-Data founder Robert Cole's influence is present in every chapter. His role is best understood as "editor in charge of clarity." If you find yourself puzzled over meaning here or there, it is probably because we did not take Bob's advice. We also thank Bob for his patience and flexibility with our ever-changing writing deadlines. He generously adjusted his schedule whenever possible to accommodate ours.

At SUNY Press over the course of this project, we thank former director Priscilla Ross, Jenny Doling, and Jane Bunker for their encouragement and support. Publication of this book completes the SUNY series *Restructuring and School Change,* which Priscilla initiated, edited by H. Dickson Corbett and Betty Lou Whitford. We are grateful to SUNY Press for the continuing support of the series and the addition of this book to it.

Of course, this book would not have happened at all without the generosity of the Lucent Technologies Foundation and the support of the Philanthropic Initiative. Hallie Tamez, senior program officer with the Philanthropic Initiative, was our primary contact throughout. Her twelve years of experience as an elementary schoolteacher showed in both her understanding and her questions. Unwavering in her commitment to improving schooling and teaching so that children benefit, she was unfailingly responsive, supportive, and insightful, asking tough questions and sometimes applying a swift boot to our collective backsides.

At the Lucent Technologies Foundation, David Ford and then Christine Park supported the initiative from their position as foundation president. Most recently, Florence Demming provided oversight from the foundation. We greatly appreciate their support.

This book, focused on collaboration, is also a consequence of it. We are especially grateful to all who contributed chapters, not only for their fine work, but also because they were willing to sit down as a group to discuss and synthesize what we had learned from involvement in this project. Bob Cole facilitated the gathering, and Florence Demming and Hallie Tamez joined us to contribute their insights. That memorable conversation considerably deepened our understanding of emerging patterns across research sites and helped us immeasurably in composing the final chapter.

We also thank Susan Lytle from the University of Pennsylvania and our USM colleagues in the Bozo's Writing Group, particularly Julie Canniff, Melody Shank, and Jean Whitney, for reading early drafts of some chapters.

Over the last five years, as we have wrestled with elusive ideas and struggled to put them into writing, the two of us have learned firsthand a central message in this book. Professional relationships and work become stronger when sustained through both encouragement and critique. We are grateful that our relationship has grown and deepened through our work, and vice versa.

The individual with whom we worked the closest at Lucent, Richard Curcio, will forever have a special place in our hearts. In 2005, Rich died. While with the Lucent Technologies Foundation, he championed grant making intended to enhance the success of public school-children and the effectiveness of adults working with them. The Peer Collaboration Initiative was one of those. Moreover, he understood, even delighted in, the unpredictable, sometimes meandering path of creativity and innovation, both as the project unfolded in the schools and in the evolving research that documented it. He was a teacher and a gentle man. We miss him.

INTRODUCTION

BETTY LOU WHITFORD AND DIANE R. WOOD

In the last decade, reference to "professional learning communities" has dramatically increased in the literature of both education and business. What, in fact, is a "learning community"? What purposes should learning communities serve? How do they operate? How do participants interact? How *should* they interact to fulfill their purposes? What motivates people to participate in them—or resist them? What is the relationship between teachers' learning communities and contemporary demands for accountability and data-based decision making? In other words, do learning communities actually contribute to improving schools and student learning, and how do we know? What conditions would convincingly attest to their efficacy? In the end, how does a learning community differ from any other group of colleagues working together?

In this book, we share what we have learned about these questions based on six years of research in a project originally funded by the Lucent Technologies Foundation, with continued funding from Alcatel-Lucent, following the merger of Lucent Technologies, based in Murray Hill, New Jersey, with a French information technology company, Alcatel. Called the Peer Collaboration Initiative, the project's first phase established professional learning communities in a set of schools in four districts in New Mexico, Washington, Pennsylvania, and Florida and, in a second overlapping phase, three districts in New Jersey. The foundation also funded two teams of researchers to document the project, provide feedback to the funder and to project participants, analyze outcomes, and engage in dissemination of the research. The authors of seven of the eight chapters in the book were members of these research teams.

The project designers intended the initiative to support learning communities as an innovative vehicle for teachers' professional development that would transform the schools' professional cultures. That is, the project's aim was to supplant individualistic and privatized approaches to teaching with a professional culture in which teachers make their practices more public and take collective responsibility for student learning. Thus within the Peer Collaboration Initiative, we came to define "learning communities" as small groups of educators who meet regularly to engage in systematic, ongoing, peer support and critique in order to improve their educational practices and student learning.

In chapter 1, the editors of the book, Betty Lou Whitford and Diane R. Wood, present two vignettes of learning communities, one highly functioning and one seriously struggling, and they compare and contrast them. In that chapter, we try to capture the complex alchemy required of learning communities so that they can foster the relational and analytic capacities necessary for teachers' learning communities to make a difference. In chapter 2, Whitford and Debra R. Smith describe the Peer Collaboration Initiative in detail and provide a summary of the experiences in the initial four school districts. This chapter sets the stage for the project, explaining its original vision and scope.

Chapters 3, 4, and 5 delve into specific district and school experiences in various policy contexts. In chapter 3, Wood tells the story of what happened in the Pennsylvania school district of "Hillsboro" and analyzes several critical issues affecting the fate of the project. Diane Yendol-Hoppey contributes chapter 4, writing about the influence of high-stakes accountability on collaborative inquiry within learning communities in "Beach County" schools in Florida. Smith, Dick Corbett, and Bruce L. Wilson formed the research team that documented phase two of the initiative, and in chapter 5, they describe the events and effects in the New Jersey districts.

In chapter 6, Wood parses and analyzes in detail the meaning of "professional," "professional learning," and "professional learning community." In chapter 7, Ken Jones reflects on the first six chapters, exploring purpose and ends and larger societal pressures on schools, raising concerns about social justice and equity. In the concluding chapter 8, Wood and Whitford explore why fostering teachers as professionals offers the best hope for ensuring student learning, summarizing how learning communities can contribute to professionalizing teachers' work.

Although the authors collectively provide an unflinching portrait of the struggles and limitations of teacher learning communities, they do not eclipse the hopeful promise of these communities. In our last chapter, we argue that learning communities in schools and districts characterized by hierarchically determined goals and directives seem to encourage more compliance than innovation. And yet, in rare instances, when given enough autonomy and time, learning communities did contribute to teachers taking an increasingly professional stance toward their work. Although learning communities may be insufficient in and of themselves as a means for professionalizing teaching cultures, they can make a considerable contribution toward that end, an end we argue is essential to the kind of schools our children need for the future.

PROFESSIONAL LEARNING COMMUNITIES FOR COLLABORATIVE TEACHER DEVELOPMENT

BETTY LOU WHITFORD AND DIANE R. WOOD

In the last decade, reference to "professional learning communities" has dramatically increased in the literature of both education and business.[1] Much of this literature claims that professional learning communities are a major strategy for improving institutions in a changing world. For example, in *Professional Learning Communities that Work*, Dufour and Eaker (1998) argue, "The most promising strategy for sustained, substantive school improvement is developing the ability of school personnel to function as professional learning communities" (xi).

Schools must cope with changes—either ongoing or projected—in the U.S. economy and in student demographics. They are affected by increasingly sophisticated technologies, media, and communication systems. In order to ensure that their practices are relevant and effective in the face of such sweeping changes, it is essential that adults in schools be learning continually. Since learning is fundamentally a *social* process (Belenky et al. 1997; Dewey 1997; Vygotsky 1986), teachers need to work in collegial communities that encourage sharing expertise and problem solving; building collective knowledge and exploring relevant outside knowledge; providing critique on existing practices; and inventing, enacting, and analyzing needed innovations. In these ways, learning communities become productive sites for the professional development of teachers, as well as critical leverage points for profound change in school cultures and much-needed whole-school change.

1

Thus proponents claim that schools must become "learning organizations" (e.g., Darling-Hammond and Sykes 1999; Dufour and Eaker 1998; Fullan 2006; Hargreaves 1994; Senge et al. 2000). Unfortunately, there is a stunning lack of clarity about what actually is being proposed. A wide variety of distinct professional development approaches, school social groupings, and change and improvement strategies appears in the literature labeled "professional learning communities." What, in fact, is a "learning community"? What purposes should learning communities serve? How do they operate? How do participants interact? How should they interact to fulfill their purposes? What motivates people to participate in them—or resist them? Do these communities actually contribute to school improvement and improve student learning, and how do we know? What conditions would convincingly attest to their efficacy? In the end, how does a learning community differ from any other group of colleagues working together?

In this book, we share what we have learned about the aforementioned questions based on five years of research in an initiative funded in 1999 by the Lucent Technologies Foundation. Called the Peer Collaboration Initiative, the project established "Lucent Learning Communities" (LLCs) in a set of schools in four districts in New Mexico, Washington, Pennsylvania, and Florida. (In a second phase, the foundation funded a district in New Jersey.) The project designers intended to provide and support an innovative vehicle for teachers' professional development. Within the Peer Collaboration Initiative, we came to define LLCs as small groups of educators who meet regularly to engage in systematic, ongoing, peer support and critique in order to improve their educational practices and student learning. To scaffold their efforts, the LLCs used a priori guides (known as protocols[2]) to structure their conversations as they shared professional practices and artifacts of student learning.

In chapter 2 we describe in detail the Peer Collaboration Initiative and the research we conducted. Here in chapter 1, to illustrate what we mean by "learning community," we present two vignettes drawn from our field notes of direct observations. Throughout our documentation process, we were guided by Flyvbjerg and Sampson's (2001) conception of "social science that matters," that is, research that aims to contribute to practical wisdom about human welfare—and we can think of few institutions that offer more toward the common good than public schools. With that in mind, we intend for the two vignettes to shed light on the practice, problems, and possibilities of teachers' learning communities, particularly because such communities are so often invoked as the means of improving student learning.

The first vignette is from a highly functioning LLC; the second is from one far less developed. Through points of comparison and contrast, we seek to accomplish three purposes. First, we illustrate key features of the learning communities we studied. Second, we provide a common text for readers that can be used as a point of reference in later chapters. Third, we conclude the chapter with a discussion of what these vignettes imply about ways to foster and sustain teacher learning in the community.

A LINCOLN ELEMENTARY LLC

The following vignette depicts a meeting occurring about seven months into the life of this particular learning community. The LLC is composed of six fifth-grade teachers at Lincoln Elementary, one of two schools serving students in the district's lowest socioeconomic neighborhoods. Lincoln enrolls about 700 students from diverse racial and cultural backgrounds. The teachers meet twice a month for two hours. While all have between two to four years' experience as members of an LLC, this is the first year that this group has met. And, while the facilitator has four years' experience as an LLC coach at Lincoln, this vignette occurs during her first year working with this group. On this day, the participants experienced a breakthrough. For the first time, a teacher brought an example of a student's work with her and candidly confessed frustration in working with that student.

It's a gloomy February day at Lincoln Elementary School, one of the poorest schools in this East Coast, mid-size urban district. In a second-floor classroom, a group of six teachers gathers around a table cluttered with food, coffee cups, pop cans, and papers. Speaking over the animated laughter and chatter, Alice, a teacher serving as coach for the group, speaks up, "Okay, we'd better get started. I just want to remind you of our norms, especially number one." She grins and then gestures toward a poster propped up on a bookcase. It reads:

1. *Be punctual.*
2. *Be honest. Give constructive criticism and listen to constructive criticism.*
3. *Share the air. Give everyone a voice.*
4. *Stay on topic. Use time efficiently.*
5. *Try to reach an equitable consensus when possible, but report all voices and opinions.*

6. *Be prepared.*

7. *Be flexible with norms by revisiting them from time to time.*

Voices hush. Alice continues, "Okay, Mary Ann, you're presenting today. Remember you've got five to ten minutes to describe your dilemma. We'll listen and we won't interrupt. Then we get a crack at asking some questions for about five minutes or so. After that, Mary Ann listens and we discuss the problem. Then we'll debrief. You know the drill, right?" She gestures to an easel holding a chart. The chart reads:

<u>Protocol</u>

Presenter presents dilemma (10 minutes)

Clarifying questions (5 minutes)

Probing questions (5 minutes)

Discussion (15 minutes)

Presenter responds (5 minutes)

Debrief the process (5 minutes)

Mary Ann begins, "Since fall, I've been trying to create a kid-friendly rubric. You know, one that makes my expectations clear? I'm using math exemplars from past versions of the state tests with the kids as in-class assignments. I don't know if these test questions are realistic for some kids, but I suppose I'll never know unless I try hard to help them. Anyway, I'm hoping to get this group of kids better prepared than last year's. I'm pretty frustrated, though." Mary Ann has launched the group into its work.

"I brought this example of one kid's work. As you can probably see, he's trying to solve one of the exemplars. [She distributes copies of a mathematical word problem that entails being able to sort out relevant and irrelevant information and analyze a simple graph.] It's typical of what happens when some kids work on these problems. You can see there's more guessing than estimating. You can also see that he's not quite sure which information from this word problem he needs and which information is just beside the point."

Mary Ann goes on to provide more detail about why the student's work had troubled her. Eventually, she says, "I need to figure out what to do here."

The five other teachers lean forward, listening carefully. One says, "So do you have a particular question you want us to consider with you?"

"Oh yeah, I forgot about the question. Well, let's see. I guess I want to know, 'How can I create a kid-friendly rubric that shows kids what is expected of them?'"

Alice speaks up at this point. "Since I'm the facilitator today, I want to remind everyone that we can take several minutes for clarifying questions."

Jeff pipes up immediately, "You say this is typical. How many of the kids are struggling like this kid?" Over the next few minutes, the group peppers Mary Ann with questions to put her dilemma in a clearer context. "How much experience with problems like these had you given the kids before you assessed them?" "Have you laid out the steps for the kids?" "Have you asked them to explain their problem solving to each other?" The questioning continues, until Jean asks, "Since this is a word problem, have you thought about how much your student's reading level might be affecting things?"

Before Mary Ann can answer, Alice jumps in: "We've sort of organically moved into probing questions. So, if it's okay with everyone, let's start asking the probing questions. You know what I mean. These are the questions to help Mary Ann to look more deeply at what's going on here. We've got five minutes. Go for it." Jean repeats her question. Mary Ann responds, "Well, I certainly check out reading scores and take that into consideration, but in lots of cases, I don't think that's the real problem."

The questions come slowly at first but then gain momentum:

"Have you asked the kids to think aloud as they work through these problems?"

"Are you having the kids work together on any of these, so they can talk about how they're trying to solve them?"

"Do you think this kid really 'gets' the concepts involved here, or is he just trying to go through a memorized procedure?"

"Do you think you've given enough scaffolds to support this kid's problem-solving process? Do you know if he's got some misconceptions about how to solve this kind of problem?"

"Do you give the kids a chance to look at their work afterward and revise?"

Mary Ann answers the questions and takes occasional notes. At times, she answers a question quickly and decisively. At others, she looks surprised or puzzled. Occasionally, she winces and smiles painfully. A little more than five minutes into the process, Alice announces, "We need to move to discussion." Mary Ann pushes her chair back from the table, signaling her role as a listener rather than participant. The group begins their discussion.

"I think it's important that Mary Ann gathered these exemplars and that she's trying to help kids be successful," says one teacher. Another responds, "I agree, and the fact that she chose this particular exemplar shows she's got high expectations for kids."

After a brief silence, someone remarks, "I admire her for bringing a student's actual work here. It's hard to share a sense of failure, you know?" Alice good-naturedly quips, "Yeah, leave it to Mary Ann. She's always the first one in the door—ready or not!" They laugh.

"You know I can't get the reading aspect of this out of my head. I wonder if Mary Ann worked with small groups of kids and had them read the problem aloud if it might help her. Oral reading can sometimes show you a lot."

"Okay, but her question is about a rubric. Remember she said she wanted kids to be clear about her expectations?"

"I know, but if part of what you have to do to solve a problem like this is read with comprehension, then shouldn't that be a criterion on the rubric?"

"So how's having that on a rubric going to help a kid who's struggling with reading? You can have all kinds of rubric criteria, but what good does it do?"

"Wait a minute! Are we getting rubrics mixed up with something else here? Maybe Mary Ann's not looking for a rubric here? I don't think this is really about making expectations for a final product clear. I think what this is really about is helping kids know how to think through a problem like this. It's almost like she wants a checklist to help kids with the mental process. Aren't rubrics for assessing products?"

"Maybe you're right. What Mary Ann is really asking is how to give kids a way to think about this kind of problem. Maybe a rubric could actually do that. She wants the kids to monitor how they're thinking about the problem, right? I keep going back to reading comprehension, though. It's so central to all this."

Mary Ann's colleagues discuss her dilemma from multiple angles, turning it over like a prism in the conversations, looking for insights and possible strategies. Alice remarks, "I keep wondering if the kids need a lot more practice. This problem actually requires kids to sort out a lot of relevant and irrelevant information." Jeff jumps in, "I agree. And I'm thinking about that idea I brought up earlier. What if the kids could do these exemplars in groups and explain their thinking out loud? Wouldn't they get better at doing it on their own?" Lisa replies, "Actually, this whole discussion has me wondering how I might rethink my own approach to giving kids these practice problems. I want to figure out how to help the slow readers understand the problem so I can separate out the difference between reading skills and math skills. I guess I'm in the same boat as Mary Ann. Seems like the same kids keep struggling, you know?" Alice responds, "Yeah, and how do you help those kids without boring the others out of their tree?"

"Listen, the more I think about this, the more I'm convinced we need to integrate our literacy instruction with math instruction. When kids 'get' these problems, they've grown by leaps and bounds in reading comprehension, don't you think?" Mary Ann writes furiously and, by turns, frowns with concentration or grins in delight. Throughout, she is silent. After ten minutes or so passes, Alice says, "Well, we're running out of time. Let's have Mary Ann tell us what she's heard."

"Wow! All I can say is that was amazing! I've got tons of good ideas!" Mary Ann responds enthusiastically and then enumerates suggestions and questions she plans to pursue. She ends with, "Of course, you were completely off the wall on some things. [Everyone laughs.] I mean, some suggestions you made just aren't my style and some just wouldn't work with my kids. But one thing that's really clear to me now is that my question wasn't right. What I really want to know is how to scaffold kids' thinking on problems like this."

At this point, the whole group debriefs. The group talks about the process and then Alice asks, "Did Mary Ann raise anything here useful for all of us?" In the course of the discussion, they decided:

- They have made an important distinction between thinking about rubrics as criteria for success and rubrics as descriptors for thought processes (meta-cognition).
- They have articulated more precisely what it takes for a student to tackle word problems like those on the state tests.
- They have reminded one another about an unavoidable intersection between reading comprehension and math word problems and suggested a better integration of reading and mathematics instruction.

As they enumerate what they are learning together, Lisa says, "You know, we are all really worried about what kids are thinking as they try to problem solve. Let's face it: reading comprehension is also a big worry! How can we know how to help students if we don't think through more systematically how reading affects so much else that they do and if we don't know what they're thinking? In fact, reading is all about thinking, right?"

After a thoughtful lull, Alice responds, "Whew, this has been intense. I think we owe a lot to Mary Ann for bringing student work. I want to suggest something. Remember last summer [referring to coaches' training] we learned about that idea of a 'cycle of inquiry'? The idea about our whole group working on a common question? I think we may be ready for that."

Jeff asks, "How does it work again?"

"You know, you decide you've got a question; you decide on some action plan to explore the question; you go back to the classroom and try whatever you decided to try; then you basically see if it worked; and then you come back together, talk about it and tweak it, or try something else. Or sometimes you just find a new question. I've got a chart somewhere about this. I'll dig it out."

The bell signals that time is up. The teachers jump from their chairs, grab another bite of food or sip of coffee, and snatch up their papers. Alice calls out as they head off to meet their students, "Listen, next meeting let's see if we can draw out a common question from our work today." And, in fact, for the rest of the year, they did indeed investigate the cycle of inquiry.

ATTRIBUTES OF THE LINCOLN LLC

The above vignette contains a number of qualities that distinguish it from conversations that typically occur among teachers. In other words, this is not business as usual. Some of the qualities include the following:

- adopting an inquiry stance
- acknowledging limits of individual knowledge
- making individual worries public
- tightly focusing on teaching and learning
- collectively committing to ensuring student learning

Adopting an inquiry stance. There are a number of points in the discussion where teachers could simply have resorted to excuses. For example, they could have said, "These kids can't read, so how can they do word problems?" Someone might have added, "These tests aren't realistic for our kids." But rather than becoming mired in conditions they viewed as beyond their control, the group members began looking for ways to address the problems at hand and then posed a number of questions. The presenter began with questions, but more were raised during the ensuing discussion by other participants. All involved adopting a stance of inquiry (Cochran-Smith and Lytle 1993, 2001), turning over in their minds their colleagues' dilemmas as they thought about possible strategies. The community's deliberations generated multiple possibilities rather than focusing simply on a single solution or plan for solving the problem.

Acknowledging limits of individual knowledge. Because the work of teaching is ostensibly about bringing knowledge to students, many teachers want to project an air of expertise. When they are unsure of subject matter or frustrated by an inability to reach students, they often feel guilty and scramble either to find some answers on their own or to cover up the deficit. In the previous vignette, however, teachers talked openly about "not knowing" how to teach reading in conjunction with mathematics, and they revealed to one another doubts about how to help their students with word problems. They demonstrated clearly that being a competent teacher does not require knowing everything. On the contrary, competent teaching requires owning up to "not knowing" and engaging in continuous learning.

Making individual worries public. A closely related factor is that when one teacher openly admits a lack of knowledge, then others are freed to do so as well. Typically, teachers are not only highly reluctant to reveal what they do not know, but they are also often reluctant to ask for help from their colleagues. During this meeting, for the first time in the life of this group, a teacher brought a student work sample to her colleagues and made a plea for help. In doing so, she took the group beyond a sustained commitment to meet regularly. Her action helped the group embark on a deeper endeavor: to make thorny dilemmas public in the group and to engage in systematic, focused discussions about addressing them. By bringing an authentic teaching and learning problem to her colleagues, Mary Ann demonstrated her faith that useful professional knowledge resided in the group. When group members actually discussed the problem, they saw for themselves how much practical benefit can arise from participation in their LLC. With so many demands on their time, teachers must be convinced that collaborative efforts, such as LLC work, are going to be worth the effort.

Tightly focusing on teaching and learning. With structure provided by the protocol and an experienced facilitator, and because the group is a manageable size (six teachers), the conversation stayed focused on the issue brought to the group by one member. At the same time, participants used the protocol as a guide rather than a recipe; as such, it shaped the discourse but did not interfere with its fluency. Although participants remained focused, the discussion also took interesting detours from the presenter's question. While these detours generated new possibilities in terms of defining and addressing the problem, participants did not stray from the central issue: improving student learning. The substance of the discussion was clearly professional, but relationships also seemed to thrive, as evidenced by the easy laughter and gentle gibes. The vignette captures teachers doing serious work while also enjoying each other's company.

Collectively committing to ensuring student learning. Perhaps most important, these teachers are clearly concerned with how to help students. Faced with the work of a struggling student, they do not waste time delineating the student's inadequacies as a learner and bemoaning the supposed causes. Rather, they try hard to analyze precisely what difficulties the student is encountering so that they can generate strategies to help him or her surmount them. The heart of the whole conversation reveals an abiding faith that the student can and will learn if classroom conditions are right. This vignette also reveals the willingness on these teachers' part to shoulder the responsibility for ensuring students' learning, even those who struggle the most. It demonstrates that teachers in this LLC never resort to defining students as hopeless. Instead, they embrace their students' learning struggles as problems to be solved.

A SANTOS ELEMENTARY LLC

The example of the Lincoln teachers demonstrates a group that has achieved a certain level of sophistication as a learning community. How might their LLC compare and contrast with one that is newer, less experienced, less developed? What might characterize a less sophisticated group? To shed light on these questions, we present a second vignette of a group that has been together for only four meetings. Moreover, most of the group's members are new to LLCs. As with the Lincoln LLC, the session portrayed in the following vignette from Santos Elementary was the first time the group had looked at student work from a member's classroom.

The 2001–2002 school year marked the second year of participation in LLCs for Santos Elementary, a school of approximately 500 students in a large district in the Southwest. That year, 78 percent of the faculty took part in an LLC, exceeding the initiative's expectation of 50 percent. With this rapid expansion, new groups had formed, and LLC memberships from the previous year had shifted somewhat.

Most LLCs in this district followed the format used in the coaches' training: sessions opened with "Connections," a time for group members to share personal stories and thoughts. The group then reviewed feedback from the previous session, revisited the group's norms (established during the first meeting of the group), and engaged in an icebreaker activity as a way of building trust. Commenting on these opening activities, one experienced coach observed, "It's a way to have fun and destress and to make us comfortable while we make our practice public."

In the remaining time, the group would use a protocol, facilitated by one of the group members, to structure discussion of a particular reading, professional dilemma, observation of one another's practice, or, as in this second vignette, to guide examination of teacher and/or student work artifacts brought to the group by a member. Near the end of the LLC sessions, the participants would fill out "reflection" forms, which encouraged them to comment on the session and their experiences, as well as suggest what might be done in their next session. While many groups in this district reported frequent use of a protocol for discussing professional dilemmas, which does not require attention to specific student work samples, a few LLCs had started bringing student work samples to their meetings.

The following vignette is from the fourth meeting of the group, held in December. At Santos, the LLCs met once a month, from 1:50 p.m.–4:20 p.m., on a day when students left early in order to provide a block of time for teachers to work together.

Conversation and occasional laughter increasingly fill the air as twenty-one teachers gather in a classroom, sign in, and pick up snacks from a long table against one wall. The noise subsides at 2 p.m. as soft-spoken Maria opens the meeting with the group's routines. First, there is "Connections," followed by a review of reflections from their previous meeting, a revisiting of group norms, and an ice-breaker activity. Just after 3 p.m., the teachers form three small groups, each with a designated facilitator, and begin working with a protocol. Maria, now facilitating one of the small groups, announces that they will be using the "ATLAS— Learning from Student Work" protocol.[3] Reading from a handout she is holding, she informs the group of the characteristics of the nature of their work together, as expected by the ATLAS approach:

- *Looking at student work cannot simply be adopted as a technique by schools or teachers, but must be learned over time in a thoughtful, supported way.*
- *Time should be provided for a discussion of the purposes for using a particular process or approach; time should be reserved for reflecting on ("debriefing") the process just completed.*
- *Looking at student work demands blocks of time for teachers to work together, from an hour and a half to a full day.*
- *Looking at student work will be more effective when sustained over time, for example, year-long monthly or twice-monthly meetings.*

Without any discussion of these points, Maria passes out copies of the protocol and asks the participants to review it silently. An unusual feature of this particular protocol is that it directs users to focus only on the work sample and to assume that the work makes sense to the student. According to the protocol, the teacher providing the work sample "should not give any background information about the student or the student's work." The point is to use only the evidence in the work and not the teacher's expectations or judgments about the student. It describes five steps for the group's session, providing key directions and suggested questions in each along with suggested time limits:

- *Getting Started (2 minutes)*
- *Describing the Student Work (10 minutes)*
- *Interpreting the Student Work (10 minutes)*
- *Implications for Classroom Practice (10 minutes)*
- *Reflecting on the Process (10 minutes)*

When the participants finish reading, Maria introduces Rachel, a teacher in a Title I program aimed at helping students transition from special education into regular classrooms. Maria is explaining that Rachel has volunteered to present her student's work. During the first step of the protocol, Rachel deviates from it by giving some background on the student as she passes around copies of three pages from a student's journal. She explains, "This is part of a reading response activity I gave to my transition class early in the year. The student is a female in the third grade, and I've been increasingly concerned about her."

On the three pages, the student had written thoughts and drawn pictures in response to Rachel's prompts and questions about the novel Harry Potter and the Sorcerer's Stone. *Again, Rachel deviates from the protocol by talking about her expectations: "For this assignment, I was looking for high-frequency words and spellings appropriate for the third grade, and the student's ability to make accurate observations of the text and logical interpretations."*

Providing yet more background information, she adds that her inquiry question for the year is, "When should I expect desired concepts to be internalized [by students]?" As is expected of all members of the district's LLCs, Rachel has identified a question about her practice that she is focusing on throughout the year. The intention is that each LLC member will work on a unique question with the group's coach and with the other LLC members.

Maria makes no effort to limit Rachel's comments, which would assist the group in following the protocol more closely. Rather, after Rachel describes her inquiry question, Maria directs the group's atten-

*tion to the next section of the protocol, "Describing the Student Work,"
which is to last ten minutes. She explains that the teachers should
describe what they see in the student's writing samples while Rachel listens and takes notes but does not speak. She emphasizes, "Be very
descriptive, without making judgments or interpretations."*

*Comments from the participants, offered with periods of silence in
between, demonstrate that the teachers find it challenging to refrain
completely from interpretation and judgment:*

> *"The student uses a variety of font sizes in her writing."*
> *"The pictures are simplistic, but defined."*
> *"She appears to have difficulty with capitalization and spelling."*
> *"She uses complete thoughts."*
> *"The student shows knowledge of subjects and predicates."*
> *"The student shows comprehension [of the text] through the
> use of expanded sentences."*

*The identification of characteristics continues for nearly twenty min-
utes, with participants remarking on the "wobbliness" of the letters, the
way the student closely followed the margins on the page, and the types
of pictures she drew, which one teacher finds to be expressive and animated. A number of comments focus on grammar. One participant
points out that the student tends to overgeneralize the "ck" phonetic
cluster, another points out "consistency in spelling," and another notes
that the "commas are where they are supposed to be."*

*During this time, Rachel increasingly squirms in her chair, shifting
her body position while appearing to listen intently. Eventually, she
blurts out, "This is hard!" She then explains that she is finding it very
difficult to remain silent and not jump in with explanations or in
defense of her student. As facilitator, Maria is nondirective, making no
moves to keep the teachers focused on the elements of the protocol or
to point out that they are mixing judgments with descriptions.*

*Glancing at her watch, she says, "Okay, we'll now move to the
third part, 'Interpreting the Student Work.'" Again reading from the
handout, she explains, "It's where we'll attempt to make sense of what
the student was doing and why, by finding as many different interpretations as possible and evaluating them against the kind and quality of
evidence." She points out that Rachel is again expected to listen, take
notes, and not talk.*

*Much of the ensuing discussion is nonresponsive to Maria's direc-
tion and centers instead on the student's understanding of grammar,
accentuating the positives the group members see in the work. They
comment that "the student has a good grasp of verb tenses," "a good*

sense of punctuation," and makes "good use of proper nouns." Again they have strayed from the purpose of the protocol by diagnosing the child rather than imagining the child's thinking. At one point, Rachel muses aloud, "She does have a nice voice and rhythm in her writing."

The next segment of the protocol directs the group to focus on implications for classroom practice. Maria reads aloud that the group is to "discuss any implications this work might have for teaching and assessment in the classroom." The group members become more animated and make suggestions about how Rachel could help her student. One suggests that Rachel construct a flowchart of the plot of Harry Potter that the student could keep in her journal. Others ask: "Have you tried having the student read assignments out loud, you know, to build on her oral skills?" and "Have you done any peer editing with the kids?" Rachel replies, "No, they don't do peer editing—the group isn't there yet." Another suggests, "How about putting examples of the student's work on an overhead projector, so the class as a whole can revise and edit it." Another cheers Rachel on with, "You do have her writing now. She's on the right track. She just needs polishing for presentation."

Neglecting the final segment of the protocol, "Reflecting on the Process," Maria announces, "We're now at the end of the protocol." Rachel jumps at the chance to talk about her student: "There's this thing with spelling with this student. She gets perfect scores on her spelling tests, but I'm really worried about this kid. She has a speech impediment and has trouble pronouncing her 'r' blends. She consistently scores one to two levels below grade level on reading tests." Appearing to reflect on what she's heard from the group members, she muses, "You know, this kid is more interested in telling a story, not writing."

Rachel's insight is left hanging as the allotted time is over and group members begin packing up their materials, preparing to leave. Maria comments, "How difficult every kid is." Another says, "I can't imagine doing this for a whole day."

COMPARING SANTOS AND LINCOLN

The preceding episode from an LLC at Santos Elementary reveals some characteristics in common with the more experienced group at Lincoln. In both groups, a teacher is willing to share artifacts of work from her own classroom and appeal for help to the members of her learning community. Moreover, both presenting teachers exhibit a willingness to trust the group to provide needed help and appeal to them with questions based on a student work sample. Both groups stay focused on the intended topic; while their conversation is guided by a protocol, neither group strictly adheres to each step.

In addition to these common features, there are important differences, and some of the common features have different effects. The Lincoln group displays fluency and comfort with the conversation, even as it raises questions and issues. The facilitator's guidance is seamless, attending to the flow of the conversation more than directing it, with no clear demarcations of the beginning and ending of the phases of the discussion.

In fact, the teachers at Lincoln appear to have internalized the steps of the protocol and adapted it to their needs. Teachers other than the presenter express their own worries as they offer suggestions and ask for clarification from the presenting teacher.

At Santos, in contrast, only the presenting teacher names a problem or issue. There are few opportunities for clarification, and the somewhat stilted discourse proceeds haltingly, as if the teachers are unsure of the process. Their talk becomes animated only when they are prompted to offer implications for classroom practice, perhaps indicating less comfort with what the protocol asks of them until the end, when they feel in more familiar territory.

The Santos facilitator appears less skilled, allowing multiple deviations from the protocol. For example, when the presenting teacher obviously violates the protocol by describing her intentions and interjecting information about her inquiry question, the facilitator does not interrupt or redirect her. The group is not guided into discussion of the considerable evidence they have generated, and the insight Rachel voices at the end about the student being more interested in storytelling than writing is left dangling, a lost entry point for collective knowledge development and teacher learning. And, alas, the group will not meet again for a month.

Among the many possible reasons for the observed differences between the two learning communities, three stand out. One is simply that "experience shows." Not only does the coach at Lincoln have four years' experience in that role, but each of the learning community members is also experienced in LLCs (two to four years each). Moreover, Lincoln's group has been together for seven months and meets twice monthly for two hours. In contrast, the Santos vignette is from that group's fourth meeting, a session that occurs only once a month. The coach is newly trained, and the members have no prior experience using protocols.

A second explanation is size and structure. The Lincoln group is small—only six teachers—while the Santos group of twenty-one is much larger. Even as this large group breaks up halfway through the meeting for more intimate protocol-guided conversations, it is not clear that the membership of the small groups remains constant from meeting to meeting. Such lack of continuity would likely diminish their development as an LLC. The Lincoln teachers meet twice monthly for two hours, while the Santos group meetings are monthly for two-and-a-half hours. A month between conversations, especially when participants are novices at peer critique and assistance, is less likely to contribute to the development of analytic discourse than would more frequent meetings. Another structural feature is how the two LLCs use their time together. For the Lincoln group, the analytic discussion of their professional practice is the focus of their two hours. The Santos group used only about half of its time together in this way.

A third explanation for the observed differences is in the choice of protocol used by each group. The Lincoln group used what is commonly referred to as the "consultancy" protocol. The steps of this popular format are very familiar to the group, so much so that its discussion flowed rather quickly and purposefully toward more analytical discourse. The protocol guides group members, but they easily find their own footing and spend most of their time in substantive analysis and thoughtful reflection on the nature of the problem they are considering. In fact, it's conceivable that the group, at that point, could have had the same discussion with very little reference to a particular protocol. Earlier practice with the protocol had taught the teachers how to have the conversation, and their experience led them to focus on analysis.

At Santos, even though the facilitator read aloud the assumptions behind the "ATLAS—Learning from Student Work" protocol, there is little evidence that those assumptions had significance or meaning for the group. The needed conditions set by ATLAS include sustained use over time, thoughtful support, time for discussion of purpose, and reflection on the process. None of those conditions obtained. Thus there was a significant mismatch between the circumstances of that particular learning community and what was needed for effective use of the protocol. Therefore, while both groups deviated from the protocols they used, the deviations at Lincoln extended the analysis and furthered a shared purpose; at Santos, the deviations altered or subverted the intentions of the protocol's designers and did not result in the intended analysis.

Moreover, of the two protocols, the ATLAS protocol is likely to be more challenging to use effectively. ATLAS directs teachers to learn from student work by suspending judgment and being strictly descriptive about the work without prior knowledge of context—about the teacher's expectations, or the classroom setting, or the student. Such a stance is highly counterintuitive and also runs counter to other pressures on teachers to learn as much about individual students as possible. Thus not only are the Santos teachers engaging in a new practice—examining the work of a student from one of the teacher's classes—but they have selected a protocol that directs them to do this in a novel and perhaps an uncomfortable manner. The Lincoln teachers are also examining student work for the first time. However, even though they are far more experienced with peer critique, they use a protocol they know well to guide their dialogue.

CONCLUSION

The two vignettes highlight characteristics we saw both in newly formed LLCs and in LLCs that developed over time with the individuals and groups supported by the Peer Collaboration Initiative. For a variety of reasons (e.g., shifting research focus, school district personnel changes), we do not know how that particular Santos learning community evolved. We do know what happened at Lincoln, and that story is contained in chapters 6 and 7.

As the initiative developed, we observed that certain practices more than others accompanied teachers' insightful analytical discussions about teaching and learning. Through engaging in constructive criticism, participants grappled with *problem posing*, with understanding the nature of the problems and issues they brought to the group rather than simply with solution seeking. Along with the many suggestions for addressing problems or issues, group members also wrestled with the multiple perspectives within the group. Along the way, new roles developed—teacher as critical friend, teacher as problem poser, teacher as learner, teacher as inquirer—that overlaid their many other roles, including teacher as implementer of imposed mandates and responder to external accountability.

And when their work together really "cooked," they began to build a *shared responsibility* for developing knowledge with each other about teaching and learning. They became *accountable to each other* for what was happening in their own classrooms as they tried out ideas generated in the group and shared with group members their tales of success (or of woe).[4] Their work together became highly meaningful for their work with their own students.

We are convinced, however, that if teacher learning communities are to reach their full potential to leverage significant change, then such communities must do even more. The teachers participating in them—and the leaders of schools, and of school districts—must reject recipelike answers to complex problems, which are all too often proffered in schools. They must come to see that constructive responses to children's learning problems demand keen attention, not only to generalized ideas about research-based practices but also to the specific, the idiosyncratic, the relational, and the personal. The Lincoln LLC shows us glimpses of what it looks like when teachers search together for contextualized answers to contextualized problems.

In the best of the communities we observed, teachers' shared observations about students were rich in detailed particulars about behavior, attitudes, and social contexts. Out of their talk rose complex portraits of their students—their words, interactions, and behaviors. Moreover, in these communities the collaborative dialogue spawned possibility, inventiveness, and hope. Instead of hovering tightly around "the ways things have always been done" or "are we doing the protocol right?" the teachers' conversations took flight toward what could be and what ought to be.

If this vision for teachers' learning communities were to become widespread reality, then teaching might become something more than a "special but shadowed" (Lortie 1975) semi-profession. Learning communities can contribute to the true professionalization of teaching by increasing the likelihood that good teachers will stay in teaching, professional learning will be enhanced, and teachers' tacit knowledge and practice-based expertise might be leveraged for the greater good. Teachers, then, would be positioned to reclaim accountability as a professional right and responsibility. The purpose of the rest of this book is to explore both the possibilities and the realities that arise from teachers learning in community. In exploring the multiple dimensions of this complex work, we have remained optimistic, even in the face of so much to lament over many of the current public policies governing teaching and public education in America.

NOTES

1. For example, a literature search confined to journals produced by the American Educational Research Association between 1964 and 2000 yielded 788 articles using the phrase, while a search using Google Scholar in mid-April 2006 produced millions of hits.

2. For examples of protocols, go to http://www.nsrfharmony.org or http://www.lasw.org.

3. The descriptions about the mind-set needed for this approach to looking at student work that the facilitator read to the group appear to be from the work of Steve Seidel and colleagues of Project Zero at Harvard University. These statements do not appear on the actual protocol the group used during its December 2001 meeting. That document contains a note saying it is a tool developed by Eric Buchovecky and draws on the Project Zero work and that of the Leadership for Urban Mathematics project and the Assessment Communities of Teachers project.

4. For a fuller treatment of teachers' stories, see Wood 1992, 1996, 2000. See also Wood and Lacey 1991.

REFERENCES

Belenky, M., B. Clincy, N. Goldberger, and J. Tarule. 1997. *Women's Ways of Knowing: The Development of Self, Voice, and Mind.* New York: HarperCollins.

Cochran-Smith, M., and S. Lytle. 1993. *Inside/Outside: Teacher Research and Knowledge.* New York: Teachers College Press.

Cochran-Smith, M., and S. Lytle. 2001. "Beyond Certainty: Taking an Inquiry Stance on Practice." In *Teachers Caught in the Action,* ed. A. Lieberman and L. Miller, 45–58. New York: Teachers College Press.

Darling-Hammond, L., and G. Sykes. 1999. *Teaching as the Learning Profession: Handbook of Policy and Practice.* San Francisco: Jossey-Bass.

Dewey, J. 1997. *Experience and Education.* New York: Free Press.

Dufour, R., and R. Eaker. 1998. *Professional Learning Communities that Work: Best Practices for Enhancing Student Achievement.* Bloomington, IN: Solution Tree.

Flyvbjerg, B., and S. Sampson. 2001. *Making Social Science Matter: Why Social Inquiry Fails and How It Can Succeed Again.* New York: Cambridge University Press.

Fullan, M. 2006. *Learning Places: A Field Guide for Improving the Context of Schooling.* Thousand Oaks, CA: Corwin Press.

Hargreaves, A. 1994. Changing *Teachers, Changing Times: Teachers' Work and Culture in the Postmodern Age.* New York: Teachers College Press.

Lortie, D. 1975. *Schoolteacher: A Sociological Study.* Chicago, IL: University of Chicago Press.

Senge, P., N. Cambron-McCabe, T. Lucas, B. Smith, J. Dutton, and A. Kleiner. 2000. *Schools That Learn: A Fifth Discipline Fieldbook for Educators, Parents, and Everyone Who Cares about Education.* New York: Doubleday Dell.

Vygotsky, L. 1986. *Thought and Language.* Cambridge, MA: MIT Press.

Wood, D. R. 1992. "Teaching Narratives: A Source for Faculty Development and Evaluation." *Harvard Educational Review* 62:4: 535–50.

Wood, D. R. 1996. "An Inquiry into North American Dreams." *JCT: An Interdisciplinary Journal of Curriculum Studies* 12:2: 39–43.

Wood, D. R. 2000. "Narrating Professional Development: Teaching Stories as Texts for Improving Practice." *Anthropology and Education Quarterly* 31:4: 426–48.

Wood, D. R., and C. Lacey. 1991. "A Tale of Teachers." *National Women's Studies Association Journal* 3:3: 414–21.

ॐ 2 ॐ

CREATING LEARNING COMMUNITIES

The Lucent Peer Collaboration Initiative

BETTY LOU WHITFORD
AND DEBRA R. SMITH

A s the Lincoln vignette in chapter 1 demonstrates, analytical conversations among teachers about student work and their own teaching practices can have powerful effects. Teachers' knowledge—ordinarily tacit and individually held—is elicited, shared, and critiqued. New roles and practices emerge, new insights develop, teacher learning is enhanced, and deeper understanding about individual students' learning and the connections to teachers' practices is developed. At the same time, as the Santos vignette in chapter 1 makes clear, these effects are not arrived at quickly or easily.

How did the learning communities portrayed in chapter 1 come into being? How did they become situated in their districts? What supports were provided? How did the initiative evolve? What accomplishments and tensions developed as the project unfolded? In this chapter, we address these questions by describing the multiyear Lucent Peer Collaboration Initiative and how the research team interacted with project leaders and participants. The chapter concludes with a summary and discussion of the effects of the initiative across the initial four participating districts.

TEACHER LEARNING THROUGH PEER COLLABORATION

In 1999, the Lucent Technologies Foundation set a particularly ambitious goal when it supported an initiative aimed at transforming the professional cultures in a set of schools through new approaches to professional development. The centerpiece of the initiative would become "Lucent Learning Communities" (LLCs)—small groups of educators meeting regularly to engage in systematic peer critique and support by sharing their own professional practices as well as artifacts of student learning. The foundation engaged The Philanthropic Initiative (TPI) to develop and manage the project and the National School Reform Faculty (NSRF) to train teachers and administrators in the approach and to support the districts' efforts. Educators in twenty schools in districts in New Mexico, Washington, Pennsylvania, and Florida were the initial participants. In a second phase, Lucent funded school districts in New Jersey to engage in a redesigned version of the initiative.

Lucent also funded researchers—initially based at Teachers College, Columbia University, and later at the University of Southern Maine—to document the project as it unfolded and to provide ongoing feedback and advice to project leaders, the districts, and the foundation. The researchers characterized their work as "documentation" to emphasize their role as formative rather than summative evaluators. One team focused on New Mexico, Washington, Pennsylvania, and Florida, while a second team later conducted research in New Jersey. This chapter draws extensively from the work of the first team, described in more detail later in the chapter. Chapter 5 is devoted to the project in New Jersey. Figure 2.1 displays the initial project participants.

LAUNCHING THE INITIATIVE: COACHES' INSTITUTES

As project planning progressed during the period 1999–2000, TPI invited nine districts to apply for Lucent funding, intended to support three subsequent years of work. Following an extensive review of professional development practices and leadership orientations in the districts, as well as consultation with NSRF leadership, TPI and foundation staff selected four districts for awards. District leadership determined the specific schools that would be involved. In some cases, the selected schools formed a curricular or attendance pattern; in other cases, school principals volunteered their schools' participation.

Beginning in August 2000, and over the next two years, NSRF designed and facilitated four multiday institutes aimed at preparing

Fig. 2.1. *Peer Collaboration Initiative Participants*

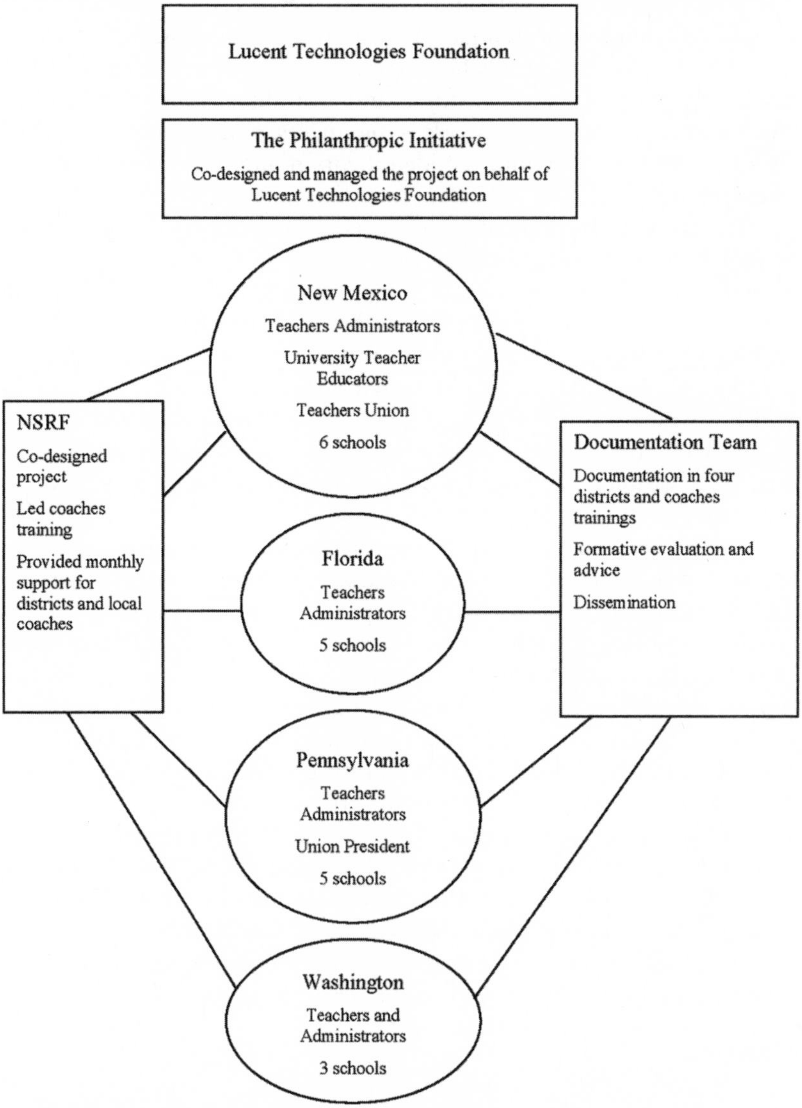

Lucent Technologies Foundation

The Philanthropic Initiative
Co-designed and managed the project on behalf of
Lucent Technologies Foundation

New Mexico
Teachers Administrators
University Teacher Educators
Teachers Union
6 schools

NSRF
Co-designed project
Led coaches training
Provided monthly support for districts and local coaches

Documentation Team
Documentation in four districts and coaches trainings
Formative evaluation and advice
Dissemination

Florida
Teachers Administrators
5 schools

Pennsylvania
Teachers Administrators
Union President
5 schools

Washington
Teachers and Administrators
3 schools

teachers and administrators to serve as coaches of LLCs in their home districts and otherwise support the initiative. Each institute was held near one of the four districts in turn, with two cohorts of teachers and administrators attending paired summer and winter institutes. These

institutes were highly structured, intensive experiences where participants worked in cross-role and cross-district sessions, learning to use
specific collaborative techniques for community building, trust building,
collaborative inquiry, group facilitation, giving and receiving feedback,
discussing professional literature, and critiquing classroom artifacts
(such as samples of student work, assignments, and classroom activities)
for evidence of quality and for identification and discussion of alternative approaches.

The institute sessions were co-directed by members of the National
School Reform Faculty, a group that formed in the mid-1990s to promote the use of "critical friends groups" as a vehicle (according to one
of the early NSRF leaders) "for building collaborative school cultures,
making professional practice public, and enhancing critical reflection on
practice, all with the aim of improving student learning." Six of the
NSRF institute trainers also served as external coaches for the districts.
In that role, they facilitated planning sessions with district teams at the
coaches' institutes and, during the subsequent school years, they provided on-site support on a monthly basis.

The project design called for the phasing in of LLCs in participating
schools over a three-year period through both the coaches' institutes
and monthly district visits by the external coaches. Leaders of the first
coaches' institute intended it to serve several purposes: (1) It would
introduce key district leaders, principals, and teachers to LLC values,
norms, structures, and processes through cross-role and cross-district
seminars. (2) The external coaches would facilitate district planning for
how the initiative would function during the period 2000–2001 in the
participating schools. (3) It would prepare a sufficient number of
coaches so that 25 percent of a participating school's faculty could be in
a group with a trained coach during the period 2000–2001. While project leaders emphasized that participation in an LLC should be voluntary, they also expected that the experience would compel at least 50
percent of each school's faculty to be in an LLC by the second year, and
100 percent by the third year as NSRF trained successive cohorts of
teachers and administrators as coaches.

DISTRICT IMPLEMENTATION

During the academic year following the first coaches' institute in 2000,
the newly trained coaches began convening and facilitating the required
number of LLCs at least once a month for two and a half hours. In

most cases, participation by teachers during the first year was voluntary, as project leaders expected, but in a few instances school administrators required teachers to be part of an LLC, so the number of groups exceeded expectations. In at least one high school, the administration required the entire faculty to meet in LLCs during the first year of the project. Finally, the three schools in the Washington district had 100 percent participation from the beginning, because they had already been convening small groups of teachers for various professional activities and folded LLC work into the meetings of those groups.

The external coaches began their monthly visits to the districts, meeting with new local coaches (called internal coaches), principals, and district staff. Serving as liaisons to project managers at TPI, they also worked to align district and LLC practices with project expectations. When variations from the expectations surfaced, TPI worked flexibly with district leaders, aiming to preserve the intent of the project while also taking into account districts' existing professional development and school improvement strategies.

One variation from the plan that surfaced early in the project was when and for how long LLCs would meet. The project leaders had asked district leaders to support meetings during the school day at least monthly for two and a half hours. However, when the groups began meeting in the fall of 2000, the pattern varied widely across schools and districts. Some LLCs met weekly during shorter planning times rather than monthly for more extended periods; others met after school rather than during the school day. In a few cases, groups within the same schools met during the day, while others met after school.

To share updates, manage the variations, and coach each other's work in the districts, the external coaches and TPI leaders held frequent conference calls. TPI also maintained regular, direct contact with district leaders and with the researchers through telephone calls, letters, reports, e-mails, and site visits.

During the second year, a new cohort of coaches from each of the project schools in the four districts—mostly teachers this time—attended a summer institute in July 2001 and a winter institute in January 2002. These institutes were again facilitated by NSRF members serving as external coaches and augmented by other NSRF trainers—some but not all of whom had staffed the previous round of institutes. In the districts, the number of groups expanded greatly—in most cases exceeding the goal of 50 percent participation in each school. The external coaches continued their monthly site visits, and the documenters continued the pattern of data collection that they had established the first year.

By the third summer of the project in 2003, the project leaders decentralized the coaches' training, shifting it from national to district-based institutes facilitated by both NSRF trainers and coaches in the districts, an expression of the local capacity building in which the project engaged.

With some exceptions where teacher participation was clearly mandated, the "voluntary but compelling" strategy for establishing LLCs appeared to work as envisioned. Survey data collected in the fall of 2003 from coaches and participants indicated overwhelmingly positive responses to the LLC experience. Over the course of the project, new groups formed and met regularly using NRSF strategies for peer interaction, so that by the third year, nearly all teachers in the original twenty schools were engaged.

Moreover, three of the four districts used local funds to create groups in additional schools. Some project leaders, excited about this development, saw it as a strong endorsement by district leaders of the value of LLCs. At the same time, at least one NSRF external coach worried that the rapid expansion would stretch the capacity of relatively inexperienced coaches to engage in skilled facilitation. There is some evidence that this in fact may have occurred, as illustrated in the Santos LLC depicted in chapter 1, where novice coaches attempted to lead groups in examining student work.

DOCUMENTATION RESEARCH

In the summer of 2000, at the beginning of the project, TPI, on behalf of the Lucent Technologies Foundation, invited an evaluation proposal from the National Center for Restructuring Education, Schools, and Teaching (NCREST) and the National Commission on Teaching and America's Future (NCTAF)—both then based at Teachers College, Columbia University. To inform the development of the proposal, senior researchers from NCREST and NCTAF attended the initial NSRF coaches' institute held in New Jersey that August; they observed sessions and facilitators' meetings, interviewed key participants and leaders, participated in some of the activities, and later submitted a proposal to Lucent. In November, Lucent made a two-year commitment to a formative evaluation of the project, indicating that an additional two years of funding to support continued documentation, writing, and dissemination might be forthcoming.[1]

Between January 2001 and December 2003, a lead documenter for each district collected data during multiday visits at least twice a year, and sometimes more frequently. During these visits, researchers spent time in participating schools where they interviewed principals, teachers, and coaches—sometimes observing classroom instruction, LLC sessions, and project-related meetings; visited district and teacher union offices to interview key central office and union leaders; and collected relevant documents. Lead documenters and research assistants also attended the four NSRF coaches' institutes, observing small- and large-group sessions as well as NSRF planning sessions and debriefings. Data collected in these ways were supplemented by telephone interviews, conference calls, participant evaluations and reflections completed during project sessions, e-mail correspondence, district reports and proposals, and external coaches' reports. During the fall of 2002, an extensive survey of LLC participants and coaches in all four districts supplemented the qualitative data.

The researchers comprising the documentation team had significant experience conducting research grounded in public schools as well as working as K–12 educators and leaders in education reform efforts. From the beginning, the stance of the researchers was that of "critical friends"—supportive outsiders who believed that the "big idea" of the project (teachers having regular opportunities to critique and support each other's practices) held great promise for positively affecting teacher and student learning. The team also periodically offered insights and suggestions aimed at improving the efficacy of the initiative. With team members located in Florida, California, New York, and Maine, the researchers held conference calls and met twice annually (in addition to being together for the semi-annual coaches' institutes) to report on individual progress and offer peer critique, as understandings of the successes and challenges of the project and the documentation in each of the districts developed.

By the team's third face-to-face meeting, in November 2001, Hallie Tamez, the TPI project manager, who had twelve years' teaching experience, began participating in the documentation team's meetings in the dual role of project manager for the foundation and knowledgeable educator committed to the project's success. Over time, her role became that of "critical friend" to the documentation team. Toward the end of the second year of documentation research, Richard Curcio, vice president of the Lucent Technologies Foundation (also a former teacher), began attending documentation team meetings as both a critical friend and project sponsor.

In the fall of 2001, the team produced a "first-look" report on the initiative that they shared widely among project and district leaders, sponsors, and coaches. The documentation to that point indicated that, structurally, the initiative was proceeding as designed—that is, the schools had created LLCs that were meeting regularly and using strategies learned at NSRF institutes. Participants mostly reported a high level of satisfaction with the coaches' institutes and the initiative itself, with comments such as, "This is the best professional development I've ever had," and "Provides tools needed for problem solving and increasing student learning." Others expressed appreciation but less optimism about the project's power to resist "business as usual" or outside mandates. For example, one participant observed, "It helps morale but doesn't affect teaching." Another, referring to accountability pressures, offered, "It's asking us to think when we're being told what to do."

This report also pointed to potential issues, including the readiness of LLCs to examine student work; the reluctance of institute leaders to deal with challenges (e.g., how to facilitate contentious discussions of equity and diversity) in favor of celebrating successes; and evidence of multiple, competing agendas between and among the groups and district leaders, foreshadowing a likely collision of the democratic design of the LLCs with school districts' entrenched patterns of hierarchically distributed power, authority, and control.

SUMMARY OF DISTRICT EXPERIENCES

By April 2003, the research team had developed draft case reports on how the initiative had fared in each district. As anticipated, it had become situated differently in each of the four districts.

In New Mexico,[2] the staff of a school/university/union partnership developed the district's original proposal and viewed LLCs as a way to strengthen teacher professional development from preservice teacher education throughout all career stages. Initially, LLCs were created in six schools—two elementary, two middle, and two high schools. During the second year, a third middle school joined when a number of LLC members moved to that school. Later in the project, groups were created in fifteen additional schools with local funding. University teacher educators also formed an LLC that met throughout the project, with a few student teachers participating in LLCs at their placement schools. District leaders reported envisioning using LLCs as an "umbrella" for all professional development in the district.

Responding to the initiative's expectation that groups meet during the school day, the district proposed hiring substitute teachers in order to provide such released time. In practice, however, not all of the LLCs wanted to meet during the school day, so two practices emerged: some groups took advantage of the availability of substitutes and met during the school day, while others met after school and were paid a stipend from the funds that would have supported substitute teachers. Many teachers, supported by the union, argued that participation in an LLC should be compensated. The practice of paying teachers a stipend, however, raised sustainability concerns among some project leaders, who were looking ahead to the end of external funding. This practice, coupled with local budget reductions, led administrators to make choices among competing priorities. As a result, some school principals, especially in secondary schools, encouraged teachers to engage more with curriculum development linked closely to testing rather than making LLC participation the priority. Despite these challenges (and even with the added disruptions of superintendent turnover twice during the initiative), the number of LLCs continued to expand as groups formed in more schools.

On the survey of LLC coaches and participants in New Mexico, responses were overwhelmingly positive, with respondents predicting that the impact in three to five years would be significant. On the other hand, by the end of Lucent funding, the envisioned use of LLCs as the umbrella for all professional development had not emerged. And while the number of LLCs had expanded greatly, the focus of LLC activity varied widely, with some groups engaged in peer observation and examining student work, while others remained focused on ice-breakers and trust-building activities learned in the coaches' training sessions. With rapid expansion of the number of groups, there was evidence that the newly trained coaches who were expected to lead the groups needed more support than was available in order to guide groups into a more effective analysis of practice.

In Washington,[3] the district positioned the project in three high-need schools that were to become a K–12 arts curriculum pathway. The NSRF external coach had also been an ATLAS trainer in the district and so already had an insider's knowledge of reform work that was taking place. The district committed to supporting two hours of weekly released time for teachers in all three schools from the beginning of the project and saw the initiative as fitting well with their vision of teacher-centered professional development. Teachers' survey responses in the Washington district were also very positive. As the schools' educators struggled to address low test scores, there was evidence that the external coach was the key agent in the LLC work in two of the three schools. And while the district's professional development office created standards to guide decentralized school-based strategies congruent with LLCs (e.g., the deprivatization of practice, collaboration, collective focus on student learning, and shared norms), the district's multiple district-wide reform initiatives, major budget shortfalls, and leadership turnover made it difficult for the schools to navigate priorities.

The Pennsylvania district[4] began the project in five schools, with significant participation by the district's professional development office and the president of the teacher union. The district provided time for groups to meet during the school day and, in the second year, created the role of "apprentice" to the external coach as a means of building internal capacity for taking leadership of the project within the district. The apprentice role was adopted by other districts, and individuals in those roles assisted the external coaches during the semi-annual coaches' institutes by the second round. As in New Mexico, the number of schools creating LLCs increased beyond the original group, so that by the third year, the apprentices in the Pennsylvania district led a coaches' institute for the growing number of participants from these schools.

As in other districts, survey data indicated that teachers were overwhelmingly positive in their assessments of their LLC experiences. With the strong leadership of a charismatic and an energetic superintendent, the Pennsylvania district began to institutionalize the use of LLCs by creating a sustainable infrastructure with the potential to support lasting change. As with other districts, however, the evidence indicated wide-ranging practices in terms of the depth of the work undertaken by LLCs, pointing to the likelihood of differential impact on students. Significantly, the research also revealed that the values and norms fostered by the initiative were counter to historical and cultural norms of public schooling; despite the superintendent's supportive rhetoric, this district was no different. The conventional power and authority patterns of leaders in both the central office and individual schools remained in place as the district twice experienced superintendent turnover.

The Florida district[5] situated the project in five schools in one of their district's divisions. While all districts in the project faced increasing demands for test-driven accountability, the pressure was particularly intense within Florida's high-stakes system. In addition to the NSRF external coach (who was also a teacher in a neighboring district), three professional development specialists (one from the central office and two from the division level) worked with the newly trained coaches in the five schools. The documentation research indicated that the LLCs became well integrated in several of the schools as well as at the divisional level. As with LLC participants in the other districts, Florida educators' survey responses indicated very positive reactions to the LLCs. In particular, respondents recognized the power of peer collaboration, the potential effects of focusing on student work, and the need for peer discussion and deliberation.

TEACHERS' RESPONSES AND LLC VARIATIONS

As the initiative developed, and more and more groups formed in each district, contextual variability also increased. In response to school schedules and/or group preferences, some groups met monthly for at least two and a half hours as in the original project design, while others met weekly for shorter periods of time. Group membership changed with teacher turnover and/or when teaching assignments, school schedules, or individual priorities changed.

By the third year of the initiative, virtually all teachers in the participating schools were members of a group. In many instances, particularly during the initial stages, participation was voluntary or "encouraged"; in others, principals clearly required it. On the survey, teachers' responses about the value of the LLCs were very positive, with slightly more positive responses from those who reported voluntary participation. Overall, teachers judged LLCs as having more value to their own learning than did conventional approaches to professional development; they reported that they valued highly the opportunities LLCs afforded to have professional conversations with colleagues. Also, teachers reported spending considerably more time than they had prior to joining an LLC discussing student work samples, assignments, and lesson plans with colleagues and receiving useful suggestions from colleagues about curriculum materials and problematic teaching and learning situations. Among the professional activities teachers found most beneficial were looking at teacher work (e.g., lesson plans, student assignments), looking at student work (e.g., writing samples), posing and exploring problems and dilemmas, and personal reflection. Responses also indicated a positive trend in teachers' sense of being supported by colleagues' and administrators' sense of improving their practice and trying new classroom strategies.

A significant area of variability across LLCs was the focus of their work. Based on teacher reports on the survey and researchers' documentation, some LLCs established a clear sense of purpose, with participants engaging in productive and analytic discourse about teaching and learning that affected their professional identities and practices as educators. Other LLCs concentrated more on establishing trust within the group, noting that trust was necessary before they could turn to critical dialogue about substantive professional issues. Based on self-reports, some groups did not appear to move beyond trust building. While most groups reported meeting the expected two and a half hours each month, some experienced problems scheduling time during the school day, which resulted in short, rushed meetings not conducive to thoughtful dialogue.

Another difference across groups was in how they used the NSRF protocols. During the institutes, coaches had opportunities to experience a number of protocols, copies of which were contained in large binders given to each participant as part of the institute materials. Back in the districts, some groups reported trying out a number of protocols, focusing on "doing the protocols well" rather than using them as guides to prompt meaningful discourse about teaching and learning. In some cases, groups used the same protocol every time they met, regardless of the topic under discussion. While some did not get beyond trust-building activities, others eventually abandoned the protocols altogether—either because they viewed them as constraining rather than enabling dialogue, or because other work co-opted the LLC time.

How the role of coach in the groups was enacted also varied. In the original design, coaches were specially trained for the role; in some groups, however, "coaching" effectively became "facilitation," and the role rotated among the group membership. In other groups, one designated, trained coach facilitated each session. Moreover, there was evidence of varying skill at facilitating groups, which may have played a role in shaping the focus and depth of different groups' inquiry.

How the agendas for the group sessions were determined is yet another difference that affected focus. NSRF trainers argued that individual LLC participants should set the agendas in order to enhance ownership, trust, and empowerment, as well as to enhance authenticity and democratic participation. This pattern held in many cases, especially in New Mexico, where there was no evidence that anyone outside of the groups influenced their agendas. In other cases, school and district leaders co-opted LLC time for work such as scoring students' responses on practice assessments in preparation for the state test, arguing that it served the LLC agenda. From the beginning, the Washington schools used the groups to address school-wide goals, such as raising math test scores. It is not clear from the evidence that the source of the focusing topic made a difference in how the groups functioned vis-à-vis the depth of their analysis about teaching and learning. However, this situation did lead to debate about whether or not, and how, groups could effectively address individual teacher-determined needs in the context of specific district and state accountability pressures. This point is addressed in greater depth in subsequent chapters.

LOCAL DOCUMENTATION, COLLECTIVE INQUIRY, AND PROJECT REDESIGN

While at least some of the variations may have served local needs without affecting what happened during group sessions, one could argue that other variations did have an impact. For example, when the focus remained primarily on trust building, there was less time available to develop analytic discourse about issues directly related to teacher development and student learning. Seeing so many variations, the documentation team became increasingly concerned with how to assess impact rather than merely uncovering and describing the complexities of the variations. Because the researchers visited the districts only periodically, they did not have many opportunities to get a close view of how particular LLCs were functioning over time. This concern contributed to the decision to focus the next phase of documentation on two of the four districts—those in Florida and Pennsylvania—and, moreover, to explore with those districts the feasibility of developing a local documentation strategy.

In July 2002, the documentation team hosted a two-day meeting with the TPI project manager, the NSRF external coaches, and district professional development leadership from Florida and Pennsylvania to explore together how documentation could become more collaborative between local and external researchers. The organizing question was, "What differences are LLCs making?" The ensuing wide-ranging discussion eventually coalesced around how to embed local documentation within each LLC. A critical factor complicating this direction was the fact that project leadership, especially the NSRF coaches, expected each member of an LLC to explore an individually identified inquiry question. This work was either already under way or expected to begin in each LLC during the subsequent school year.

The possibility of embedding local documentation in each LLC coincided with the researchers' perspective that having LLCs focus inquiry on a common question was likely to be more effective than continuing to pursue individualized agendas, especially in groups that met only once each month. This perspective became the focus of a second two-day meeting in December 2002, attended by those who had met in July, and expanded to include eight LLC coaches and classroom teachers. Much of the discussion in December focused on theory and methods of action research. Working intensely and diligently as a design team, the December group created a pilot project in which six LLCs would focus their inquiry on a common question generated by each LLC and document impact during the spring semester. The developments during this December meeting became known in the project as "the meeting in Maine." The result was that four LLCs engaged in sustained collective inquiry. Their coaches, the lead documenter, and external coaches for each district developed a set of papers that presented their work as an interactive symposium at the 2004 meeting of the American Educational Research Association. The details of what happened with these pilots are described in and/or inform the discussions in chapters 3, 4, and 6.

On differing time lines during the spring of 2003, the LLC coaches who participated in the December "meeting in Maine" began introducing the idea of collective inquiry and local documentation to the members of their LLCs. Concurrently, early in 2003, TPI asked the researchers to develop recommendations that could inform the redesign of the initiative, since the Lucent Technologies Foundation had begun considering funding a set of schools in New Jersey to engage in this work.

With the perspective that more effective work was just beginning to take hold, the researchers responded to the request, reflecting on the evidence to date. They noted that the literature on school change suggests that innovations typically require five years to be fully installed and sustained (Fullan 1991). In fact, Schlechty (1991) argues that many innovations wither within the first three years because the new norms posited by the innovation produce conflicts and challenges that are harder to sustain than the ways of working that characterized relationships prior to the introduction of the innovation. These conflicts and challenges were clearly evident in the districts and schools where old norms, behaviors, and structures continued to guide professional development, even as local resources were used to expand the number of LLCs in nonproject schools. District administrators' expectations for LLC activities remained unclear.

Along with these conflicts and challenges was the atypically positive reaction of teachers to this professional development experience. Unlike the fairly typical reactions to much that is done in the name of "professional development" or "staff development," teachers in this initiative clearly valued the project and the time the LLCs provided to talk with colleagues. The evidence at the three-year point was that groups had formed, they were meeting, and they were using a number of the strategies NSRF advocated.

What was *not* clear at the three-year point was the extent to which what was happening in the LLCs was actually having a positive impact on teacher development and student learning. The evidence at that point indicated that teachers in some LLCs took on new roles, developed analytical skills, and developed trust in their colleagues to generate new understandings and practices centered on enhancing student learning. However, because of the wide variations in how LLCs developed and what they did when they met, the evidence regarding the impact on students was limited. This realization led documenters to focus more closely on a few LLCs as they engaged in collective inquiry (see chapter 6).

In February 2003, as requested by TPI, the documentation team assembled a set of observations and recommendations based on the evidence to that point. These served as a starting point for discussing the redesign of the project as Lucent considered funding a set of districts in New Jersey. Two members of the research team joined NSRF trainers in a meeting hosted by TPI in February 2003 to outline the redesigned project. Subsequently, one of the original members of the documentation team became the director for the documentation in New Jersey, and two new researchers joined that team. (See chapter 5 for the summary and analysis of the project in New Jersey.) Meanwhile, documentation in Florida and Pennsylvania continued.

Some of the observations and recommendations reported to TPI in February 2003 included the following:

- The initiative should begin with a planning grant to participating districts rather than with coaches' institutes bringing individuals together who are not well versed in the expectations and demands of LLCs.
- Inevitably, LLCs collide with conventional school norms, particularly those regarding the distribution of power and authority. The countercultural aspects of LLCs should be made explicit, emphasized in trainings, and addressed in districts and schools.
- LLCs should be put forward explicitly as a reform that can help integrate other reforms, otherwise prevailing district/ school norms will position them as yet another innovation, resulting in more fragmentation rather than a shifting of professional and organizational norms.
- There is a tension between LLC members identifying and addressing compelling needs related to student learning and

professional practice, on the one hand, and school and district administrators viewing LLCs as a vehicle for accomplishing work related to organizational priorities. When and how LLCs can serve larger school reform goals needs to be addressed from the beginning.

- Challenges and conflicts generally did not occur related to goals but rather to key organizational processes, especially decision-making power and use of time.
- Internal coaches need better grounding in understanding school change. Unexpectedly encountering barriers (predictable from the research on school change), without strategies for dealing with them, promotes a sense of "premature failure."
- LLCs should cultivate habits of inquiry and the central use of tangible evidence as a process that teachers can own for continuous improvement. The process should also encourage LLCs to seek outside expertise when needed, especially related to surfacing and critiquing assumptions.
- LLC agendas can be individualized or group based, short term or sustained. There are trade-offs with each combination. Participants' sense of purpose and collaborative efficacy is strengthened by a shared focus over time rather than individualized topics that change with each session.
- Coaches' training should focus on inquiry and analysis, with protocols seen as one of many vehicles rather than as a central activity of LLCs. Participants would benefit from a "form follows function" approach in which they learn to craft and facilitate collaborative processes that engage LLCs in serious inquiry around a compelling question (identified by the LLC members) that has the power to affect student learning in meaningful ways.
- Substantial research indicates that community develops when individuals engage in meaningful shared endeavors rather than through specific trust-building activities as a prerequisite to substantive work. While LLC activities such as ice-breakers may be helpful in creating new groups and as a strategy for providing a "bridge" for participants to shift their focus from other responsibilities to the work of their LLC, they should not be a central activity.
- School and district leaders need to understand how LLCs can support professional development aimed at enhancing student

learning and be able to provide support in the form of time and resources to sustain groups' work.

- LLCs need time to take hold. Districts, funders, participants, and documenters all need to recognize that shortcuts are unlikely.
- Each school needs to have a critical mass of internal coaches. The coaches require support from the principal and the opportunity to meet and develop their understandings over time. Mentoring of new coaches by more experienced ones is also important to sustaining and strengthening the work of LLCs over time.
- Administrators need to understand the significance of continuity and stability. In order to focus on analytic discourse, LLC membership should remain as stable as possible, or at least not be reconfigured each year. Ideally, the size of groups should be small (ten or fewer); groups should meet more frequently than once a month, with each session scheduled to provide adequate time for engaging in reflective discourse.

Subsequent chapters discuss many of these issues in more detail. At this point in the initiative, the Florida and Pennsylvania districts received an additional year of Lucent funding to deepen the LLC work in their districts and to plan for its sustainability. Documentation of these efforts continued into a fourth year and informs chapters 3, 4, and 6. While it was clear that participating teachers embraced Lucent Learning Communities as a valuable approach to professional collaboration and learning, the conditions encouraging the development of LLCs toward analytic discourse and new professional roles and identities were just beginning to emerge, along with the challenges of documenting the impact of the work (see chapter 6). To this point, the story of the initiative demonstrates that learning communities have the potential to enhance student learning but face a multitude of obstacles. These issues are discussed in the remaining chapters in the book.

NOTES

1. Organizational and leadership changes within NCTAF resulted in NCREST taking the lead with the documentation. Prior to these changes, Linda Darling-Hammond, Carla Asher, and Fred Frelow contributed to the conceptualization of the documentation proposal. At

NCREST, Heidi Fisher served as project manager; research assistants Ji-Sung Chong, Lindsay Stanley, and Christine Clayton helped with project administration and data collection. In the summer of 2002, the University of Southern Maine (USM) became home base for the research team when the principal investigator, Betty Lou Whitford, became dean of the College of Education and Human Development. At USM, Debra Smith served as project manager and later as principal investigator when the work extended into New Jersey. Alison Moser, Chris Backiel, Ken Bedder, Laura O'Neill, and Robin Day contributed to project management and data analysis.

2. Jon Snyder, Betty Lou Whitford, and Heidi Fisher documented the initiative in New Mexico. Whitford and Fisher wrote the report from which both narrative and data for this section are drawn.

3. Ann Lieberman was the lead documenter in Washington and wrote the report drawn upon here. Melissa Eiler served as research assistant.

4. Initially, the documenters in Pennsylvania were Betty Lou Whitford and Heidi Fisher. At the beginning of the second year of the project, Diane Wood became the lead documenter and wrote several reports that directly inform this chapter, especially the articulation of the set of recommendations at the end.

5. Diane Yendol-Hoppey (formerly writing as Diane Yendol Silva) served as lead documenter in Florida throughout the project, initially supported by Rodman Webb. This section borrows from the case report she prepared. Linda Gonzalez served as research assistant.

REFERENCES

Dunne, F., and F. Honts. 1998. "That Group Really Makes Me Think! Critical Friends Groups and the Development of Reflective Practitioners." ERIC Document Reproduction Service No. ED 423 228. Paper presented at the Annual Meeting of the American Educational Research Association, San Diego, CA, April 1998.

Fullan, M. 1991. *The New Meaning of Educational Change.* New York: Teachers College Press.

Lesser, E., M. Fontaine, et al., eds. 2000. *Knowledge and Communities.* Boston, MA: Butterworth-Heinemann.

Lieberman, A. 1995. "Practices That Support Teacher Development: Transforming Conceptions of Professional Learning." *Phi Delta Kappan* 76: 591–96.

McLaughlin, M., cited in Cushman, K. 1998. "How Friends Can Be Critical as Schools Make Essential Changes." *Horace* 14: 5.

Schlechty, P. 1991. Schools for the 21st Century: Leadership Imperatives for Educational Reform. San Francisco, CA: Jossey-Bass.

Sergiovanni, T. J., and R. J. Starratt. 2002. 7th ed. *Supervision: A Redefinition*. New York: McGraw-Hill.

Wenger, E. 1998. *Communities of Practice: Learning, Meaning, and Identity*. Cambridge: Cambridge University Press.

ᥫᦂ 3 ᦀᥫ

LEARNING COMMUNITIES

Catalyst for Change or a
New Infrastructure for the Status Quo?

DIANE R. WOOD

INTRODUCTION

By the time the school district of Hillsboro, Pennsylvania became part of the Peer Collaboration Initiative, it was already a district on the move. Immediately upon taking the helm, a visionary new superintendent began reassuring her staff and the larger community that the district would "definitely be rising" over the next few years. This was a particularly daring pronouncement; shortly before she took her position as superintendent, the district had been designated an "Empowerment District," a euphemism used by the state Education Department to put districts with low test scores on notice. In short, if scores did not go up, then Hillsboro would lose local control to state oversight.

Even as she faced the possibility of heavy state sanctions, the superintendent responded by entrusting teachers with the primary and collective responsibility for finding ways to improve student learning. The design and intentions of the Peer Collaboration Initiative were especially compatible with the superintendent's orientation to professional development. Instead of relying on traditional approaches to professional development, which draw on expertise outside of the teaching profession, she chose to embed in the district a learning community structure designed to emphasize, critique, build, and enhance practitioner expertise and efficacy. This chapter, drawn from data gathered over a five-and-a-half-year study, tells the story of what happened in the

41

Hillsboro district as a result of its decision to join the initiative and identifies several crucial issues that surfaced along the way and affected the success and the sustainability of the initiative.

Located in a historic, mid-size city in the northeastern United States, the Hillsboro School District has struggled with many of the same problems found in much larger metropolises nearby: disparities between the haves and the have-nots, entrenched poverty in some sectors, a shifting and sometimes mercurial economy, and rapidly changing demographics, largely due to recent immigration. Both enriched and challenged by diversity, the Hillsboro schools serve between 11,000 and 12,000 students—43 percent Hispanic, 32 percent Caucasian, 22 percent African American, and 3 percent Asian/Other. Like other cities in the Northeast, Hillsboro's economy has experienced major upheavals since the post-World War II boom. Once a manufacturing center, the city has come to rely more heavily on tourism and a service economy. Not surprisingly, the schools face challenges typical of other U.S. urban districts: closing the achievement gap between middle-class and poor children; developing culturally responsive educational practices to reach the children of recent immigrants, including those whose first language is not English; providing adequate resources in uncertain economic times; and meeting intensifying federal and state accountability demands.

The invitation to apply for Lucent Foundation funding came at a propitious time for Hillsboro. The state was exerting considerable pressure for higher student achievement, and the district's new superintendent recognized the project's potential to build internal capacity for change and improvement. As the superintendent put it, "I want to build capacity, and building capacity means embedding it in the work of teachers." Having secured the grant and begun working with members of the National School Reform Faculty (NSRF), the district's plan was (1) to prepare increasing numbers of Hillsboro faculty and administrators to facilitate such learning communities in their own district, and (2) to fund an "outside coach" from the NSRF to advise the district throughout the process.

This, of course, involved rethinking the traditional in-service model for professional development and instead locating it in practitioner learning communities. The district sent district administrators and teachers for coaches' training by the NSRF so they would be prepared to facilitate LLCs back home. The district superintendent promised to provide time during the school day for these communities to meet and to use project funds for crucial resources, particularly substitute teachers, books, curricular materials, meeting supplies, refreshments, and so forth. She also pledged to find ways to institutionalize and support these local learning communities after an initial three years of funding. The superintendent and her planning committee decided to begin the initiative in five schools—three elementary, one middle, and the only high school. All five schools had significant populations of students receiving free and reduced lunches. In fact, the majority population of the middle and elementary schools was comprised of children from low-income families.

Given that Hillsboro educators had been demoralized over the past several years before the arrival of the new superintendent by a series of failed change efforts and public criticism, it is telling that when the superintendent invited district leaders, teachers, and principals to participate, few turned down the invitation. Participants attributed their initial involvement to her optimism, expertise, and enthusiasm. Asked specifically about her leadership, LLC participants described her as "savvy," "energetic," "knowledgeable," and "badly needed."

According to their accounts, she swept in like a windstorm, managing to set high expectations while also raising confidence. Uncompromising in her demand that staff members shoulder responsibility for improving student learning, she also made clear efforts to provide adequate resources. As she put it, "I believe in high demand and high support." And, she had a coherent vision for change:

> I want to give us a common language and a common set of tools. I don't want cookie-cutter schools but common intellectual standards of practice. I want everyone, every school, every administrator, every teacher, and every student rising. I want all the schools there, not just a couple. I want them to be able to keep their uniqueness and creativity, but I want them to share some standards. I want to see more sharing of practice, and I know that means teachers growing the confidence to share practice. I want to see more critiquing and improving practice. The second thing I want to see is an emerging cadre of leadership, a cadre of people that you can draw on. . . . I mean by that multiple kinds of leadership focused on kids' learning.

CREATING LEARNING COMMUNITIES AS AN INFRASTRUCTURE FOR CHANGE

The Peer Collaboration Initiative evolved out of the foundational idea that teachers working in professional learning communities who share dilemmas and expertise are more likely to improve student learning than teachers working alone. Built into this notion is the idea that practitioner expertise and collaboration *matter*, and that school cultures need to be reimagined and reconfigured so that both can flourish. The initiative assembled sophisticated teams to work with the districts: NSRF consultants, local administrators and teachers, a consultant from a philanthropic organization, and university researchers. This design drew on outside and local perspectives, practitioner and theoretical knowledge, both top-down and bottom-up impetus for change, and ongoing data collection as grounds for continual reflection and assessment.

All five Hillsboro schools involved in the initiative were struggling with low student test scores; their students were among the poorest in the district. The principals and several teachers from each of the schools joined administrators from the district's Office of Teaching and Learning (OTL), and the teachers' association president, in attending the NSRF's first training sessions held during the summer of 2000 and the winter of 2001. In all, Hillsboro sent twenty-five staff members to these institutes to be trained as "internal coaches" to facilitate local LLCs.

During the training, NSRF facilitators spent much of the time providing hands-on experiences with a number of protocols designed to structure professional conversations clearly focused on the actual work of students and teachers. Although the protocols taught during the training serve different purposes, they mostly orchestrate specific conversational stages in an attempt to focus attention on improving classroom instruction and student learning. In interviews, NSRF facilitators later explained that the protocol structure is meant to make participation in professional conversations equitable and productive, despite the severe time constraints ubiquitous in schools. Ultimately, the intent was to instill in educators reflective and action-oriented collaboration, as well as "a stance of inquiry" (Cochran-Smith and Lytle 2001).

Equipped with these new protocol strategies, the twenty-five newly trained coaches organized and led LLCs in the district during the following school year. While the project design called for at least 25 percent participation by teachers that first year, in Hillsboro at least 50 percent of the faculty in each of the five targeted schools (and in some schools a greater percentage) participated. The principal of the high school, also a newly trained coach, led an LLC for administrators, and OTL administrators established LLCs for instructional facilitators (IFs), classroom teachers who had been released from teaching duties and assigned to support roles in schools.

Because funding for the LLC initiative enabled the schools to hire substitutes, the Hillsboro LLCs met during the school day that first year as well as in the subsequent two years of funding. Moreover, the "outside coach," an NSRF member who lives and works in a nearby city, provided ongoing support and guidance during that time. She helped the districts' internal LLC coaches troubleshoot group dynamics, provided resources on emerging topics, and helped LLC coaches deepen their facilitation skills. Meanwhile, the three OTL administrators provided ongoing support from the district office by creating yet another LLC group dedicated to the concerns of the internal coaches.

The following summer, twenty-three more Hillsboro teachers and administrators received training as coaches in another meeting sponsored by the LLC initiative and facilitated by the NSRF. Some of those trained during the first year's summer and winter institutes returned, serving as apprentices to the NSRF facilitators in order to deepen their understanding and skills in working with protocols and to train as leaders in the initiative. Participation in the LLCs grew markedly in the five Hillsboro schools during that second year, reaching 100 percent participation in two schools.

The third summer, the district held its own institute for LLC training. According to the OTL office, the LLCs had earned by this time a widespread and positive reputation, and volunteers for the training had to be turned away because district leadership had a limited number of trained facilitators, and they wanted to maintain a 1:20 ratio between facilitators and trainees. Teachers and administrators from seven more of the district's elementary schools participated. The district contracted with NSRF to do the training; once again, formerly trained internal coaches served as apprentices. During the subsequent school year, LLCs met in all but three of Hillsboro's elementary schools, and there was 100 percent participation among teachers in the five original schools. During the fourth summer, the remaining three elementary schools and two middle schools, as well as more OTL administrators, received on-site training.

Thus going into the third year of the project, LLCs had been introduced to a majority of teachers in the district; the LLCs were poised to become the district's infrastructure for professional collaboration and school renewal, just as the superintendent who had applied for the grant had intended. She had said the following during the first year:

> Something I feel strongly about in this district—you'll hear me say it over and over again—is capacity building. We need to sustain this work over time. We need to establish an intellectual community and an inquiry-based mind-set. . . . What the Lucent initiative does for us is that it moves deeply into the teacher ranks. It builds their capacity to be inquiry based.

MOVING FROM INITIATING TO INSTITUTIONALIZING

From the beginning of the project, there was evidence that Hillsboro leaders were aiming toward institutionalization of the LLCs. For instance, the OTL newsletter for the district publicized LLC activities and upcoming trainings. When the district initiated an effort to improve formative assessments in the middle school, the district curriculum director formed a special LLC of middle school instructional facilitators. That LLC researched and discussed new approaches and eventually formed LLCs of volunteer teachers who also studied a variety of approaches, tried them out in their classrooms, and brought their experiences back to the larger group. And, significantly, the president of the teachers association participated actively in the initiative and eventually became an "outside coach" for a district in a neighboring state—a district that has joined a "second round" of the initiative. Even during the first year, NSRF protocols began appearing in meetings other than LLCs throughout the district (school faculty meetings, for instance), and the protocols seemed to have influenced not only the processes but also the substance of the meetings. In the fall of the project's second year, one principal said, "When you start thinking about using protocols for meetings, it changes what you think should be on the agenda. We're much more focused on discussions about teaching and learning now and much less into just announcing information."

Protocols, in fact, became increasingly pervasive. For example, the OTL office, with its three trained coaches, began using protocols regularly for meetings. Protocols appeared in classrooms, particularly in the three elementary schools, but also occasionally in the middle school. According to participating teachers, students and teachers used them for setting norms, text-based discussions, and building positive relationships. As the reputation of protocols spread, one principal said she was

> getting teachers coming up to me and asking, "What's this LLC thing? What are these protocols?" And then they want to know why they can't participate. If I'd told them they *had* to participate last year, they would've fought me. It kind of amuses me. But it's all because the teachers participating like it so much and it just spreads word-of-mouth.

Yet another sign of institutionalization was the fact that Hillsboro hosted its own coaches' training during the third summer, supported in this effort by four NSRF coaches. By the end of that summer, Hillsboro had accumulated a staff sufficiently well versed in protocols and facilitation that they were able to host the subsequent two summer institutes on their own. Local coaches even began making plans to extend their work to other districts in the region. From the perspective of participants, these efforts at institutionalization had wide-ranging positive effects. In interviews, both principals and teachers in all five elementary schools and in the middle school reported that teachers, due to LLC text-based discussions, did more professional reading. According to one principal, "We have become a school of readers, and the reading is changing our practices." Moreover, in the project's third year, 218 participants and 33 coaches participated in a survey conducted by the documentation team. Participants reported that they were engaging in more collaborative conversations because of the initiative. They reported the following: receiving more feedback on professional performance from colleagues; receiving more useful suggestions to improve their practices from colleagues; hearing more collegial feedback on their lesson plans and assignments; engaging in more discussions focused on student work; and getting more collaborative support for dilemmas of practice.

Moreover, the survey data indicated that trust among professional colleagues was increasing, educators were growing in their ability to meet student needs, and the district climate was becoming increasingly conducive to risk taking and innovation. Those surveyed rated LLCs more effective than other district professional development, and they believed that LLCs would continue to make a difference in the future. The external coach put it succinctly, "Collaborative practice is definitely becoming part of school culture in the district, and people are seeing the power in that."

The five principals of the target schools, echoing this enthusiasm for the LLCs, said they believed collaboration had the potential to build leadership. They argued that when teachers work together successfully, particularly when they have the opportunity to name their own professional problems and address them, they develop a sense of efficacy. "The LLCs create teacher leaders," reported one principal, who went on to explain, "One of the LLC participants was the kind of guy who went into his classroom and did his thing—very dedicated. But now he's a leader—a quiet leader, but a leader." The external NSRF coach concurred, "This work produces a whole new layer of leadership." Seeing these benefits, a district administrator remarked, "Our goal ultimately is to root *all* professional development in LLCs."

While the prospects for sustainability of the LLCs looked strong during the project's third year, there were conditions that served to undermine the LLCs as catalysts for change. Those conditions included (1) the multiplicity of change initiatives undertaken by the district, (2) uncertainties and misunderstandings about the underlying purposes and basic processes of the LLCs, including use of protocols, (3) contradictions created by embedding a teacher empowerment vehicle—the LLCs—in the hierarchical power and authority structures of the district, and (4) the question of the initiative's resiliency given myriad and predictable obstacles to school change. Each of these conditions is discussed in the following sections of this chapter.

A DISTRICT OPEN TO AND READY FOR CHANGE

Along with the LLC initiative, the Hillsboro School District was undertaking other change efforts. The goals of various initiatives focused on standards-based curriculum and assessment, multicultural education, subject-matter knowledge, parental involvement, school climate, student literacy, and English-language learners. Though not exhaustive, this list offers a glimpse into how much was going on in the district.

The five principals of the original schools recognized that the LLCs and widespread use of protocols could be harnessed to facilitate change efforts on several fronts. They began to find ways to piggyback various other change initiatives on the LLC project. For instance, the district high school—in the midst of designing standards-based curricula and restructuring the school into small learning communities—mobilized LLC participation to help with both. The high school principal provided the rationale:

> We want people comfortable working in teams. We want the school organized into teams. We're trying to embed the idea of working together right into the school structure and then build it into the schedule. The LLCs really work well for building that sort of community and then for looking at student work. We've been able to take a standards-based protocol from another grant and use it in our LLCs. . . . That's one of the reasons I like this professional development model. It's flexible.

The protocol to which the principal above refers was developed by another organization to help teachers look at assignments and assessments through the lens of standards-based education. This demonstrates how LLCs were being integrated into other change initiatives and serves as an example of a move toward the institutionalization of LLCs.

Hillsboro administrators made good-faith efforts to minimize the stress and upheaval caused by changes on so many fronts. They took pains to convey a cohesive and motivating vision for improving student learning, and, as in the case just mentioned, they tried to link reform initiatives. Signs abounded that the strategy was working. In several schools, faculty members used LLC meeting time to analyze data produced by the district's new strategies for assessing student work. In an elementary school, attempts to spark more parental involvement included an LLC for parents. In that same school, LLC energies focused on another school-wide goal: improving children's literacy. In yet another school, LLC meetings provided opportunities for faculty to inquire into problems concerning troublesome adolescent behavior and lack of motivation.

Ironically, while the district's openness to change ushered LLCs into the schools in the first place, that openness also created impediments. In interview after interview, principals, internal coaches, the external coach, OTL administrators, and other participants reported feeling overwhelmed by the press for change on so many fronts, particularly because of intense state scrutiny. Standardized test scores had become a constant focus for measuring the district's improvement and were, in many teachers' minds, the high-stakes impetus for most change initiatives. According to one teacher, an LLC participant, "The tests make us feel like we have to run faster and faster, and there's so much to shore up in the kids' learning and just not enough time."

Under these trying conditions, some coaches, trying to respond to multiple reform agendas, despaired over learning how to use all of the protocols. One principal said, "It's hard to go deeper in this [LLC] work, to really *get* how to use these protocols to improve kids' learning. It becomes a matter of just trying to master the protocols—to remember what's there." One internal coach concurred, "Look, all teachers love resources, and I'm one of them. But look at this thing [gesturing to a large four-inch binder]! It sits on my shelf accusing me." There was wide consensus among the teachers and principals interviewed that a lack of time and a blurring of focus made it difficult to sufficiently develop a command of the protocols.

Others suggested that the sheer volume of change efforts had another subtle and disempowering effect on teachers. For instance, a teacher from the high school remarked, "It gets so frustrating always being on the receiving end and not on the decision-making end of all these great ideas to change things, and it seems like there's a new idea every month." Another high school teacher explained further, "These things have come and gone, and it's sort of dependent on the district or the administrators what the latest priority will be and whether or not it will last. Most don't!" Three years into the project, an internal coach from an elementary school declared the following:

When one change after another keeps hitting the teachers, instead of feeling like we can really do something about improving kids' learning, the teachers just start looking *even more* over their shoulders to find out what they're supposed to do. It's sort of a "what's-coming-next" mentality because so much is happening. And you just end up looking to the higher-ups to tell you what you need to be doing. And here we're supposed to be figuring out how to solve some of these problems in the teacher ranks—in our LLCs. But actually all this change can just make people feel more dependent.

The issue of whether or not LLCs should be mandated was also understandably controversial. Because the district took the stand that LLCs offered a particularly promising form of professional development, and that every teacher ought to be engaged in continuous learning, district leadership decided to mandate participation. They tried to balance this top-down directive by assuring teachers that they would retain autonomy over their LLC agendas. In a spirit of fair-mindedness, district administrators conceded that mandatory participation raised the accountability level not only for teachers but also for the district. As one OTL administrator said, "Once 100 percent participation is established, we have a special obligation to provide necessary resources for teachers to continue their groups and make them effective."

Not surprisingly, however, mandating 100 percent participation inevitably raised conflict (Fullan 2002). In some Hillsboro LLCs, resistant faculty members were coerced to join enthusiastic participants. As Achinstein (2002) explains, political tensions exist not only between collaborative groups and those outside but also within the groups themselves. And clashes within the LLCs did develop. As schools moved from voluntary to 100 percent participation, some had to reconfigure groups and reschedule meetings. According to participants, some LLCs became unwieldy in size and, because everyone was involved, were forced to meet outside of school hours. One middle school participant said her group had gone from a membership of eight to nineteen, making it "much more difficult to have serious conversations about student work or our assignments or anything else." One of her colleagues explained further:

We have about twenty people in our groups. A lot of times people just start complaining and we get stuck. And once they get started, it's hard to get them off. Our present group is very resistant. And now we don't have a choice about being in an

LLC and you have to stay until 4:15 and people don't want to be here. . . . The group last year was fantastic. We brought dilemmas. Our learning support building model came out of our LLC work last year. But this year, we're just not there yet.

An internal coach in the middle school echoed the frustration, "After all that community building and trust building last year, I feel like we're back at square one."

Both teachers and administrators frequently praised the flexibility of the LLCs, particularly their ability to tap into teachers' professional interests and needs and get them fully engaged in efforts to improve student learning. Paradoxically, this flexibility could also cause problems. For understandable reasons, district leaders wanted to capitalize on any opportunity to build synergy among various change efforts already under way. The middle and high schools, for example, were involved in reorganizing their student bodies into small learning communities, each of these led by teams of teachers; at the same time, they were organizing professional development around LLCs. Meetings for LLCs and meetings for the learning community faculty teams proved to be too time consuming. Leaders in both schools decided to disband the cross-grade-level and subject-area LLCs, which had been designed to build understanding and community across the traditional boundaries that isolate teachers. Instead, they decided to use the LLC format and processes to organize the learning community faculty teams. In other words, the small learning community faculty teams became LLCs. The protocols, leaders contended, would work just as well with the faculty teams and serve the ultimate purpose of getting faculty together to improve teaching and learning.

On the surface, this seemed like the most sensible thing to do, but it had serious downsides, particularly because teachers were not consulted. Some teachers, excited by the LLC structure they had learned about during their training, complained about the LLCs losing an all-school focus. Others felt coerced by the top-down decision making, and some mourned the loss of community that had been built in their LLCs the previous year. Quite a few teachers complained that they were being asked to do too much within a limited time frame. They argued that it was not possible for newly structured LLCs to respond to the daily, nitty-gritty demands of running the learning communities and also pursue the original purposes of the LLCs—such as discussing teaching dilemmas, looking at student work, critiquing assessments, and so forth. Moreover, in five participating schools, the time that had been allotted for LLC work changed. Those schools moved from multiple

meetings every month to extended once-a-month meetings. The participants in those schools unanimously claimed that a month-long interval
between meetings was *too* long and impaired the work of the LLCs.
Although the basic structure of the LLCs—groups of teachers meeting
regularly and using protocols to structure conversations—remained
intact, the "spirit" of the LLCs (a structure that would allow teachers to
surface, name, and explore learning and teaching problems on their
own terms) seemed lost.

As principals grouped teachers in different ways to work with different reform efforts, some teachers could not understand the justifica-
tion for working with certain colleagues, a phenomenon not uncommon
to initiatives such as this one (Hargreaves 1991; Little 2002; McLaughlin and Talbert 2001). Subject-matter specialists, for instance, could not
see the value of collaborating with counselors or other specialists (P.E.
or art teachers, for instance), and vice versa. Administrators were prone
to underestimate how such traditional boundaries as grade level and
academic content tend to divide teachers' affiliations and focus
(McLaughlin and Talbert 2001).

The difficulties of building collegial communities might also have
been underestimated (Achinstein 2002; Hargreaves 1991; Little 1990,
2002). Several district administrators and one principal said in interviews that they hoped LLCs would instill in teachers habits of working
with one another that eventually could work effectively with *any* group
of colleagues. One principal expressed her fear that LLCs could simply
become havens for beleaguered, complaining adults grateful for a safe
place to unburden themselves. She put it this way, "It can't be about just
build a group, build a group, build a group, and build a group. Yes, it's
good to build a comfort level, but this is so you can move on to discuss
the things that need to be discussed about kids' learning." A district
administrator concurred, "We need to get to the point that you can use
these protocols and have these conversations whenever you're with colleagues—no matter who they are."

Perhaps both administrators are right, but the NSRF emphasized
community building in many of its protocols for solid reasons. In many
school cultures, teaching is independent, not collective, work (Cohn and
Kottkamp 1993; Little 1990; Lortie 1975). Teacher talk in the typical
faculty lounge rarely approaches the kind of professional conversations
that the protocols are meant to evoke. Collaboration becomes difficult
to negotiate amid the myriad forces that partition teachers from one
another, that is, subject areas, grade levels, complex schedules and
responsibilities, and so forth (Hargreaves 1991; Little 2002; McLaughlin and Talbert 2001). Long characteristic of schools, these kinds of

norms cannot be altered in the absence of trusting relationships that encourage risk taking and openness and that seek out and establish common ground. Such common ground is essential so that collaborative work can be purposeful and useful. To imagine, in this very early stage of the initiative, that teachers would learn techniques from their LLCs that would simply transfer to any other collaborative work was, at best, wishful thinking.

Nevertheless, some administrators in the district did make a strong case that the building of relationships ought to happen in tandem with the work of improving teaching and learning. Miller (1986) has argued convincingly that the cultural labor involved in creating harmonious and productive relationships—often the type of work most associated with women—is frequently sublimated and invisible. And yet, as Wenger (1998) explains, collegial learning occurs around multiple and interrelated dimensions that embrace both practice and community. Hence, deliberate attention needs to be paid to both. If the professional community is to be strong, then it must advance the work of improving classroom practice and student learning. And in order for that work to progress, the community must bond around common commitments, values, and achievements.

The deep communication, inquiry, and critique intended by the LLC initiative seemed inseparable from the quality of relationships in the professional culture. One principal said, "Building LLC communities opens people to change in a non-threatening way." According to the high school principal,

> it develops a common language and common experience. I'm seeing collaboration across the grade levels, and we arranged our groups in such a way that they're representative of all the grades with some specialists. People are understanding each other's practice like they never have before, but it's because they learn to feel safe with each other. They build trust. They find a purpose. That builds more trust.

This principal was on to something. The LLCs whose work was truly focused on student learning rejected the dichotomy between building relationships and accomplishing work. Participants recognized how vulnerable educators can feel in discussing, analyzing, and critiquing everyday practices in a collegial learning community, especially those practices that were not working well for students. They also saw that a significant way to reduce that vulnerability was to establish openness and trust among members of the learning community. Finally, they recognized that attempts to build trust and openness without a focus on collective professional commitments simply devolved into superficial small talk without real focus or purpose and without the power to evoke passionate and collective commitments.

OUTSIDE EXPERTISE: THE NSRF AND THE PROBLEMS AND POSSIBILITIES OF PROTOCOLS

As previously discussed, the NSRF brought protocols to the district as a way to structure collegial conversations. Of the internal coaches and participants interviewed, all expressed appreciation for how the protocols kept professional conversations focused, reflective, and productive. During a focus group, a participant said the following:

> The biggest positive thing the protocols do is to get colleagues talking and having conversations. That's the best thing. By having a protocol around the conversations, it keeps us on task and we stay on task.

An internal coach from the high school agreed:

> I've had a wonderful time with the protocols. They're beautifully structured. I think sometimes when you're doing them, they're frustrating. But in the end when you look at them, they've helped you focus. What they encourage is that they have most people sharing. Rarely do you have someone opting out. And no one's taking up too much air space. You stay on track. I tend to resist these kinds of things, too, but I do think these protocols work.

The protocols proved to have the capacity to evoke critical reflection and dialogue. An example of this capacity occurred in one of the original participating elementary schools. The internal coach brought a child's work into her LLC, work that she perceived as particularly substandard and "disturbing." Using a protocol for studying students' work, the group began to "see lots of things the boy was actually working on and what he was trying to do." Instead of attending only to what was wrong, the protocol helped the group identify means of engaging the learner.

Without exception, those trained by the NSRF as coaches repeatedly praise the quality of their experiences. It was not unusual to hear, for example, "This LLC training is the best professional development I have ever experienced." Such reactions may be, in part, because NSRF facilitators "made their facilitation transparent" and taught new coaches to do the same. In the parlance of the NSRF, this means that facilitators explain the reasons behind their decisions as they move the group along. Their aim in doing so was to demystify leadership and promote leadership skills in others.

As the NSRF member who served as an external coach consulted with the internal coaches, she asked them what they wanted to accomplish and helped them choose protocols on that basis. At one point, she adapted a protocol to help a group undertake systematic ongoing inquiry. She called the protocol I-MAP, a paper-and-pencil method for LLC participants to record a question and an action strategy to explore it, chart what they learned as they implemented the strategy, record reflections on their learning, consider how they might translate their learning into practice, and raise more questions in order to continue the process. According to internal coaches, her support was crucial, particularly as she helped them plan and think through agendas, troubleshoot interpersonal problems, and locate outside resources. Moreover, in creating this particular protocol, the external coach demonstrated that protocols in general are not ends in themselves but rather tools for larger purposes.

Interestingly, however, much of the NSRF approach to "transparent facilitation" concentrated on the how's rather than the why's of facilitation in small learning communities. Unfortunately, coaches appeared primarily concerned with conveying the rationale for procedures or "steps" in the protocols but not the rationale for the learning communities themselves. Too many of those trained by the NSRF perceived participation in LLCs as merely the faithful following of procedures. Too few understood that participation in LLCs could be a coherent, purposeful way of fundamentally changing school culture. As a result, LLC participation in Hillsboro ran the risk of regressing to an old, familiar dependency on skill acquisition, which historically has characterized far too much of teachers' work (Schon 1983). Once NSRF in-district support ended, too many LLC members were ill prepared to sustain the work by mounting convincing arguments in support of LLCs and lobbying for their continuation. This, of course, did not bode well for the initiative. *Knowing the reasons* for productive professional conversations, *understanding how dissimilar* they are to most school cultures, and being able to *articulate their value* needed to be part of what participants learned in their LLCs. Without a widespread understanding of this larger vision, LLCs could easily be misconstrued as simply a complex array of prescriptions and recipes demanding fidelity—not as a heightened level of professional judgment, as intended.

The protocols can also be problematic in other ways. As has been already mentioned, the daunting number of protocols and the wide array of uses for them proved bewildering—and sometimes overwhelming—to some internal coaches, much less to LLC participants. One coach complained:

> In the beginning, I couldn't believe how many protocols there were. It was just one after the other and I had this big binder and I was thinking I'm never going to learn all this. And even now that I'm much more comfortable with the idea and know some of the protocols and when to use them better, I still don't know half as much as I need to know to do this. I know I need more training.

A majority of coaches, when interviewed, worried aloud that they might not be bringing the right protocols to the group, or that they might not be "doing them exactly right," or that they did not have full command of them. Sometimes facilitation of learning communities seemed to be conflated with mastery of the protocols.

This issue of dependency emerged in other ways. The NSRF, knowing the dangers of getting bogged down in what cannot be controlled, advised teachers' learning communities to concentrate on issues over which they *did* have control. Ostensibly, this is sensible advice. It is futile and wasteful to spend time and energy lamenting over conditions that cannot be changed, and lamentable to allow professional conversations to devolve into gripe sessions. As one principal said, "It keeps the discussions on a higher plane, focused on kids and their learning."

Conversely, this same advice sometimes became a rationalization for strictly circumscribing the sphere of influence and responsibility that teachers were able to assume in the district's change efforts. An incident recorded during a visit to an LLC at a high school illustrates this point. Participants were discussing norms for their group. Someone said that they wanted opportunities to talk in the group about how the agenda was going to be set because there were important issues they would like to talk about, especially regarding those students who were learning English as a second language. The facilitator replied, "Look, this is our time mostly. But if an administrator tells me I have to bring something to you during this time, then I'll have to do that. That's the way it is, and that's not something we can control. We need to concentrate on what we can control." This statement was followed by widespread eye-rolling among many participants, and then by clear disengagement. Issues like these, involving power and control, run throughout the fabric of public school life (Grumet 1988; Sarason 1991). The professional jurisdiction of teachers is frequently more a matter of lore and custom than of deliberate negotiation. Thus without dialogue or investigation, some LLC teachers, hearing the admonition to consider only matters over which they had control, ceded vast areas to administrators.

Another problem arose with the lockstep sequencing and time limits of most protocols. The NSRF designed the protocols tightly to accommodate teachers' schedules, which allowed very little time for reflection and dialogue. Some participants found the protocols "restricting," "irritating," and "cumbersome." Sometimes the step-by-step processes crowded out substance. Doubtless this was, in part, due to the newness of the innovation. It took new coaches quite a while to become accustomed to facilitating the various protocols, as it did participants to engage in them.

Finally, protocols tended to lead participants toward apparent consensus without eliciting conflict. Occasionally a teacher would bring to the table a professional dilemma and ask for specific feedback. Protocols structured the conversation so that the presenter was typically either laying out the problem or responding to questions regarding it or listening to others discuss it. Very little open disagreement or difference of opinion occurred, nor were ideological positions raised and contested. An emphasis on civility provided a "safe environment" for professional exchange, but it also covered up controversial issues that lay at the heart of certain dilemmas.

In one LLC, for example, one presenter (a science teacher) opened his presentation with the claim that "kids need to know certain things." He had brought in a student's work and asked colleagues to give him feedback on how he could help the student achieve more. His colleagues discussed a few strengths in the student's paper and then gingerly challenged the presenter by asking whether the assignment had required too much memorization and too little understanding. Conceding to the presenter that some memorization might be necessary, his colleagues offered two strategies for scaffolding the student's efforts. At the end of the session, during his feedback to the group, it was clear that the presenter had really heard only the strategies to aid memorization and not the gentle suggestions to take a more constructivist approach. In other words, the larger conflict about what constitutes learning was dropped. The micropolitics of the group (Achinstein 2002), including the veteran status of the presenter and his affiliation with a high-status academic discipline, may have kept the group from pressing the central issue— that is, an authentic discussion about how students learn.

According to the NSRF coach in Hillsboro, the protocols structure conversations so that they fit a typical teacher's planning period. Because critical reflection and dialogue are core purposes for the LLCs, however, such time constraints can be problematic. There is some evidence that the hurried, step-by-step processes inherent in the protocols can actually short-circuit both reflection and dialogue. In several LLC meetings, for instance, teachers shared untested, commonsense analyses of instructional problems that cried out for background study and critical analysis, both of which were impossible within the time constraints of the protocol. More disturbing, protocols did not necessarily expose a "need to know," that is, they did not point out to participants the outside knowledge that might be needed in order to solve a problem. Too often, the protocols tended to encourage participants to wrap things up prematurely even when the topic begged for further discussion or inquiry.

A vivid example of this type of procedural shortcoming occurred when LLC participants settled on a "problem" regarding children's learning without reflecting on the middle-class perspectives that define the problem. Alarmingly, several groups allowed an unquestioned deficit view of students to dominate their discussion. An elementary school LLC, for instance, decried the "fact" that the majority of their students, most often students of color, lacked a "command of oral language," when what they actually meant was the capacity to communicate in standard English. Without getting into the politics of linguistic variations, their discussion made it clear that they were dismissing the oral language skills that many of their students brought to school. Participants failed to consider how power and privilege can "normalize" certain behaviors while rendering others deviant or marginal. The protocols, unfortunately, seemed to facilitate this rush to judgment.

Related to this problem, the NSRF has often pointed out that the work of LLCs should hinge on accepting that "there is no hierarchy of expertise." Yet this stance also, taken too literally, can be risky. This principle arises from a sincere—and badly needed—attempt to elevate the value of teacher experience and knowledge, particularly given the hubris of some educational researchers and policy makers and the gendered nature of the teaching profession in a larger society that dismisses women's experiences and knowledge (Belenky et al. 1997; Harding 1991). In fact, particular situations and problems sometimes require expertise that goes beyond practical knowledge. While practitioner expertise is undoubtedly essential to the improvement of student learning, practitioners, like all other experts, need to evaluate what they know in light of other sources of knowledge. In the process, they need to continually question their own assumptions. In other words, like the rest of us, teachers need to know both the power and the limits of their knowledge. Instead of a facile acceptance of "no hierarchy of expertise," teachers would be better served by recognizing that at given times and in certain situations, some forms of expertise may be more valuable, more needed, and more useful than others.

If these potential problems are confronted, then the NSRF has offered a form of professional development that might have the power to profoundly change school cultures and rally educators to systematically support students' learning. Some of those trained in LLC work actually made a difference in their professional cultures, helping to create unlikely alliances in the effort to improve student learning. Toward the end of the second year, one principal explained that the district

> . . . is becoming a collaborative culture. The signs are everywhere—not just in the LLCs but in faculty meetings, in the superintendent's office, in the Office of Teaching and Learning, in classrooms. It's changing us.

STRONG LEADERSHIP AND TEACHER EMPOWERMENT: WHOSE AGENDA IS IT ANYWAY?

At the time of this study, leaders at the district and building levels enjoyed, for the most part, the respect of the staff. The vision for the district's improvement seemed clear and compelling: student learning would improve if educators worked together to ensure high-quality instruction and student work that was carefully aligned with high standards. Building capacity in the district amounted to building multiple sites that encouraged leadership among practitioners. The first Hillsboro superintendent related this vision frequently in speeches and wrote about it in the district newsletter; OTL administrators paraphrased the vision in interviews and seemed to pursue it actively; and principals and teachers talked about it (and in similar terms) in their LLCs and in interviews with me. At some grade levels, in fact, even the students were talking the language of high standards. The vision, by all accounts, seemed to have taken hold and infused a can-do attitude into a formerly demoralized district.

Moreover, leaders in the district constantly reiterated the notion that "we are all in this together." There was a concerted and deliberate effort among many in the district to avoid the divisions and misunderstandings that frequently occur between teachers and administrators, building principals and district officials, and so forth. The LLC initiative facilitated this effort by creating common experiences and instilling the notion that everyone of good faith had something of value to contribute. One principal, for instance, emphasized that administrators working with teachers who are, in turn, working together are much more likely to improve instruction in their buildings:

> What I'm seeing is that we all have shared hopes now—a shared vision—that together we can make a difference for kids. It's no longer, "Well, they should have learned that last year." Now, it's that we've got these kids not learning what they should be learning and we're asking how can we get together and make this happen. And I'm not seen, as a principal, as being separate or judgmental or something. We're a team.

Past leadership, however, always casts a shadow on the present. From the perspective of some Hillsboro staff members, a multitude of change initiatives had materialized, faltered, and died over time with little input from them. Resistance to *any* form of change had taken root in some circles. One teacher, representative of those who saw district-level decisions as remote from the real work of teaching, said in an interview, "Sometimes I think this LLC stuff is just another clever way to get teachers to work together in order to accomplish the district's work." An internal coach in the high school tried to describe what he was picking up among participants in his LLC: "I know they're thinking: Is this the district just selling us another bill of goods, or is this legitimate?" Yet another teacher in the middle school said, "I hardly have time now to work with my students, and I don't have time to be in these groups if they're just happening because they're the latest fad."

Adding to the problem of acceptance was that some teachers felt they heard mixed messages about the purposes and control of the LLCs. Although the fundamental goal for the groups was always to improve student learning, the particular agendas for the meetings are supposed to be in the hands of internal coaches and participants. As a matter of empowerment and agency, if teachers are to take seriously their responsibility to ensure all students' learning, then they need opportunities to discover for themselves how collaboration can develop professional judgment and expertise. If teachers are to see district-level work and teachers' work as serving the same purposes, then they will need to have input into how district work is conceptualized and pursued. In the beginning, many administrators in the district seemed to understand this. Three of the principals, in fact, talked in interviews during the first year of the project about their decision to stay away from the LLCs, even though they wanted to participate. As one put it, "the LLCs belong to the teachers."

Nevertheless, the internal coaches, supported by reports from the external coach, said that LLC agendas were repeatedly interrupted by district work, particularly assessment-related work. This happened increasingly after the first superintendent's departure. District leaders, under pressure from the state to provide evidence of improved student achievement, worked hard to develop multiple and reliable modes of assessment so that standardized tests would not be the sole measure of success. In one school, a call to begin peer observations, one of the possible strategies LLCs can undertake, brought anxiety and resentment. An administrator explained:

> There are some people that still think this [the LLC] is a way for the administration to *force* them to be better teachers. They don't see it as they should be working to own their own improvement. It's an old belief system meeting a new one. And we have to continue to press the new one.

The new belief system to which the administrator referred was difficult to establish, however, when leadership made a practice of changing agendas and imposing new objectives for the LLCs. Although teachers and administrators ought to focus on the same work—working together so all students learn—the hierarchical nature of most school cultures ensures that administrators define and direct that work and teachers become socialized to that reality (Grumet 1988; Schon 1983). This places the real responsibility and ownership for vision and ideas on administrators and the responsibility for implementation on teachers. Thus the LLC initiative, despite the rhetoric about teacher empowerment, often masked traditional expectations for compliance and obedience.

For some internal coaches, this tension felt especially compromising. One explained:

> Sometimes there's a building issue, a discipline issue, or some other thing that intervenes. And I have to ask myself, do we stop what we're doing in order to do what is immediately needed? But most of the time I say, no, this is the agenda and this work is important. But then the day before we are supposed to meet, an administrator announces we have to do something and then I have nothing to say in it. I have to go into the LLC and look people in the eyes and say we've got to do this. And then I lose them.

Once again, related to all of these issues is the question of whether participation in LLCs is to be voluntary or mandatory. Those who resisted being "made" to join a group were likely to feel even more affronted if the group's agenda was also mandated. Volunteers felt squelched and dispirited by the resistance of the resistors. Because the district had already committed to 100 percent participation, leaders needed to think carefully about what other controls they exercised over these fledgling—and fragile—communities.

THE QUESTION OF RESILIENCY:
BREAKTHROUGHS AND BACKLASH IN SCHOOL CHANGE

Although Hillsboro made considerable headway in institutionalizing the learning community initiative, there were serious obstacles to successfully using the LLCs as a catalyst for change.

- First, high-stakes accountability policies encouraging teacher compliance contradicted the district's efforts to encourage the teacher efficacy necessary for successful learning communities.
- Second, most of the LLC groups devoted more time to community-building efforts than to critical inquiry aimed at improving practice.
- Third, the practices and principles of the initiative ran counter to entrenched norms of district culture, and the superintendent who shepherded the project in the beginning left to take another job. As a result, most of the LLCs eventually died from neglect, except for a few pockets in several district schools (see chapters 6 and 7).
- Fourth, district leaders undermined the LLCs by juggling numerous initiatives simultaneously.
- Fifth, the district did not invest sufficient authority and autonomy in LLC participants for them to take charge of their own groups.
- Sixth, and perhaps most telling, most participants could not demonstrate a clear connection between the LLC work and student learning.

While the LLC initiative ostensibly positioned teachers at the center of the reform efforts, larger cultural expectations for the Hillsboro schools focused on district leaders as the real agents of change. While the NSRF brought to the district powerful strategies for building professional efficacy and colleagueship, participants had to adapt these strategies to the cultural realities of public schooling, whose structures typically foster compliance and individualism. Sometimes the distance between adaptation and co-optation can be very small. While district leadership had strongly supported the LLCs, some district leaders' practices inadvertently awakened a backlash of resistance, misinterpretation, and regression.

On the one hand, district administrators and building principals said they wanted teachers to participate actively in the LLC initiative, eventually take ownership of it, and subsequently shoulder collective responsibility for all students' learning. On the other hand, some of these same administrators occasionally made top-down decisions that undermined teachers' faith that the LLC initiative was really meant to live up to the lofty rhetoric.

Teachers, too, were conflicted. Some teachers eagerly volunteered for NSRF training, participated in the groups, and relished the new-found sense of professional autonomy—that is, the newfound sense that teachers could make decisions, based on critical dialogue and empirical evidence, in the best interests of their students. Other teachers, however, grew uneasy with the notion that teachers might come up with their own solutions to students' learning problems. They preferred turning to experts or to those in authority. For instance, in an LLC of kindergarten teachers, at least one teacher repeatedly urged the group to consult an outside consultant before making any decisions. A teacher in a fifth-grade LLC often derailed conversations by saying, "I just wish they'd tell us what to do." Ultimately, these tensions regarding the nature of a teacher's role, sphere of responsibility, and relative autonomy threatened to subvert the initiative.

Moreover, innovations in education are famously vulnerable to shifts in leadership. Unfortunately, the superintendent who had so enthusiastically embraced the Peer Collaboration Initiative left two years after it began to take a job in another state. In that short time, she had not managed to plant her vision deeply enough in the district's culture. Even more unfortunately, her hand-picked successor left the Hillsboro superintendency after only one year amid a serious, and very public, scandal. His successor, a proponent of prescriptive curriculum programs, made her position clear by mandating basal readers and phonics programs: professional collaboration and teacher expertise were not her priorities. In many schools, the LLCs were disbanded as time for professional development was given over to training and workshops.

Perhaps most important of all, the most avid supporters of LLC participation were the teachers in particularly effective groups (see chapters 6 and 7), but they had not developed a shared language or the collective political savvy to lobby for continuing district support for the LLCs. Despite successes in some of the groups, an ambitious change effort like the Peer Collaboration Initiative is inevitably fragile, particularly in its early stages. With the departure of one superintendent and then a public scandal involving her successor, the excitement over and focus on LLCs drifted to the background. With increased pressure from the state to raise standardized test scores, the third superintendent chose to rely on "research-based" programs and curriculum packages rather than on teacher expertise. In response, many schools began reconfiguring LLCs as a venue for training teachers to use these programs and packages.

CONCLUSIONS AND RECOMMENDATIONS

One particularly exciting potential of LLCs is their capacity to build systematic collective inquiry into the work of teachers. Several of the teacher communities in Hillsboro were learning to pose a question or problem, to develop action plans, and to collect data on what happened for students as they took action. This seemed a harbinger of good things to come, but these processes were not sufficiently widespread to win over the new district leadership.

Based on Hillsboro's experience, in order for an LLC initiative to succeed, district and school leadership would need to attend carefully to the potential weak spots discussed previously and to shore them up with direct, deliberate action. Sometimes that action needs to be preemptive and preventative rather than responsive. For instance, LLC participants need (and district leaders need to understand) *why* LLCs represent a countercultural approach to professional development. All participants need a theory of action so that they approach protocols as tools and not as ends in themselves. They need to truly understand the value and efficacy of collaborative conversations and collective inquiry but also to recognize how such an approach conflicts with the hierarchical structure in most schools and districts. In the end, practitioners cannot be both malleable and acquiescent and yet also assertive and innovative in taking responsibility for student learning. Moreover, they need shared language and conviction to advocate for their collaborative work.

Participants and district leaders also need to understand the ambiguities and difficulties involved in school change. Because LLCs are not immune to forces that have stifled other change initiatives, internal coaches need to anticipate predictable barriers to change. Without such an understanding, LLCs are subject to premature failure. Both administrators and internal coaches need to be well versed in and sensitive to the ways in which LLCs might disrupt taken-for-granted expectations and ways of thinking and acting.

If teachers are truly to shoulder the responsibility for ensuring that all children learn—if they are to take ownership for the quality of teaching that goes on in their schools and to consider LLC participation a crucial means for ensuring student learning—then administrators need to avoid confounding and/or conflating the work of LLCs with other change initiatives. Many Hillsboro participants said they heard double messages about who controls the LLC agendas. Moreover, participants need to link community building more explicitly with the work of improving teaching and learning, and this needs to be done from the very beginning. Separating relationship building from collaborative work creates a false dichotomy.

During my last year visiting Hillsboro, I asked a district administrator and long-term supporter of the LLCs about their status in the district schools. Shaking his head, he said, "There are a few pockets here and there, but for the most part, they're really not around any more." When I asked another administrator down the hall the same question, she said cheerfully, "Oh, we've embedded LLC work in everything we do. We still have teachers working in groups, and we use the protocols for a lot of meetings across the district." Later, visiting one of the original elementary schools involved in the project, I asked the principal about the discrepancy in the two perspectives. She said the following:

> Yes, there are still teachers working in groups together and, yes, we still use protocols sometimes. But now the protocols are about efficiently fulfilling district objectives. It's not about collaboration and inquiry in most places any more. I get so frustrated. LLCs aren't just protocols!

The LLCs attempt to create a culture in which accountability for high-quality teaching becomes embedded in the professional culture of schools. In Hillsboro, there were and are teachers internalizing a vision of that kind of teaching and taking responsibility for trying to implement it. (See chapters 6 and 7 for extended examples.) These teachers confronted difficult problems with student learning without turning away, giving up on them, blaming others, or waiting for solutions from the outside. Instead, they turned to one another, took collective responsibility, and actively pursued effective solutions. No recipe for change could promise more than the revitalization and empowerment of those whose work directly affects what children actually experience in their classrooms—their teachers.

NOTES

An earlier version of this chapter appeared as the article "Teachers' Learning Communities: Catalyst for Change or Infrastructure for the Status Quo?," *Teachers College Record* 109:3 (2007): 699–739.

This chapter has drawn on more than five years of site visits, which included interviews and focus groups of key players, observations of LLC participants' meetings and classrooms, e-mail correspondence with several key players, observations of LLC coaches' trainings, and reviews of relevant documents. Because of previous research I had done on teachers' learning communities (Lieberman and Wood 2002; Wood and Lieberman 2000; Wood 2007), I was asked to be the outside researcher for Hillsboro. Eventually the field-based data were held in dialogue with survey data (see chapter 2) with responses from 251 LLC participants in the district.

For all but the most spontaneous encounters, the study relied on semi-structured, face-to-face interviews, using an audio recorder on occasion but most often taking notes on a laptop. I talked to the superintendent, district administrators, the teachers' association president, the NSRF outside coach assigned to Hillsboro, trained coaches who facilitated LLCs, and participants in the LLCs. In addition, I interviewed nonparticipants in two of the elementary schools. I kept in touch by e-mail with two of the coaches and the external coach, as well as with two of the district administrators. I observed two of the coaches' training sessions held during the summer, as well as subsequent meetings to review and deepen their learning with the coaches. I observed three teachers—all trained coaches—in their classrooms at two of the targeted elementary schools.

A survey was administered to all participants in the four districts involved in the LLC initiative, including those in the five Hillsboro schools during the fall semester of the initiative's third year. Total respondents included 218 participants and thirty-three coaches. Questions focused on attitudes, experiences, impact, and sustainability regarding LLC participation. Data from this survey provided a crosscheck for the data gathered on site, confirming emerging insights and occasionally providing new avenues for interview and focus group questions. As the data accumulated, patterns emerged and were recorded in research notes. I had the luxury of communicating with other researchers working in the other three districts also involved in the LLC initiative. We met or talked on the telephone periodically to compare notes during the entire process. Once the data had been collected, I settled on the following categories around which to cluster the data:

- the implementation of the LLC initiative and the construction of teacher agency
- the purpose(s) of teacher collaboration as defined by various players involved in LLCs
- the institutional impact of LLCs
- the enabling and constraining dimensions of the policy and institutional contexts for the LLC initiative

Throughout, theories in several areas—feminist (Belenky et al. 1997; Gutmann 1999; Grumet 1988; Harding 1991; Hofmann 1981; Martin 1994; Miller 1986), school change (Fullan 2002; Goodlad 1984; Hargreaves 1994; Sarason 1991, 1996; Senge et al. 2000), and critical (Apple 1995; Freire and Aronowitz 2000; Giroux 1988, 1997)—aided the interpretations discussed in greater detail later. In the process of making sense of the data, I checked in periodically—by e-mail, phone, or face-to-face conversations—with the superintendent, district administrators, the outside coach, and the principals of the five targeted schools. The superintendent, district administrators, the outside coach, two LLC coaches, and building principals of the five targeted schools read drafts of the manuscript. Moreover, the manuscript was made available to all participants in this research study.

REFERENCES

Achinstein, B. 2002. "Conflict Amid Community: The Micropolitics of Teacher Collaboration." *Teachers College Record* 104:3: 421–55.

Allen, D., T. Blythe, and G. Thompson-Grove. 2004. *The Facilitator's Book of Questions: Tools for Looking Together at Student and Teacher Work.* New York: Teachers College Press.

Apple, M. 1995. *Education and Power.* New York: Routledge.

Belenky, M., B. Clincy, N. Goldberger, and J. Tarule. 1997. *Women's Ways of Knowing: The Development of Self, Voice, and Mind.* New York: Basic Books.

Calderwood, P. 2000. *Learning Community: Finding Common Ground in Difference.* New York: Teachers College Press.

Cochran-Smith, M., and S. Lytle. 1993. *Inside/Outside: Teacher Research and Knowledge.* New York: Teachers College Press.

Cochran-Smith, M., and S. Lytle. 1999. "Relationships of Knowledge and Practice: Teacher Learning in Communities." *Review of Research in Education* 24: 249–305.

Cochran-Smith, M., and S. Lytle. 2001. "Beyond Certainty: Taking an Inquiry Stance on Practice." In *Teachers Caught in the Action,* ed. A. Lieberman and L. Miller, 45–58). New York: Teachers College Press.

Cohn, M. M., and R. B. Kottkamp. 1993. *Teachers, the Missing Voice in Education.* Albany: State University of New York Press.

Cremin, L. A. 1964. *The Transformation of the School: Progressivism in American Education.* New York: Vintage Books.

Darling-Hammond, L., and G. Sykes. 1999. *Teaching as the Learning Profession: Handbook of Policy and Practice.* San Francisco: Jossey-Bass.

Dewey, J. 1916. *Democracy and Education.* Carbondale: Southern Illinois University Press.

Dewey, J. 1929. *The Sources of a Science of Education.* New York: Horace Liveright.

Dewey, J. 1997. *Experience and Education.* New York: Free Press.

Dufour, R., and R. Eaker. 1998. *Professional Learning Communities at Work: Best Practices for Enhancing Student Achievement.* Bloomington, IN: Solution Tree.

Elbaz, F. 1983. *Teacher Thinking: A Study of Practical Knowledge.* New York: Oxford University Press.

Flyvbjerg, B., and S. Sampson. 2001. *Making Social Science Matter: Why Social Inquiry Fails and How It Can Succeed Again.* New York: Cambridge University Press.

Foucault, M. 1980. *Power/Knowledge: Selected Interviews and Other Writings, 1972–1977.* New York: Pantheon Books.

Freire, P., P. Clarke, and S. Aronowitz. 2000. *Pedagogy of Freedom: Ethics, Democracy, and Civic Courage.* Lanham, MD: Rowman & Littlefield.

Fullan, M. 2002. *Change Forces with a Vengeance.* New York: Falmer Press.

Fullan, M. 2006. *Learning Places: A Field Guide for Improving the Context of Schooling.* Thousand Oaks, CA: Corwin Press.

Giroux, H. A. 1988. *Teachers as Intellectuals: Toward a Critical Pedagogy of Learning.* New York: Bergin & Garvey.

Giroux, H. A. 1997. *Pedagogy and the Politics of Hope: Theory, Culture, and Schooling: A Critical Reader.* Boulder, CO: Westview Press.

Goodlad, J. 1984. *A Place Called School*. New York: McGraw-Hill.

Grant, G., and C. E. Murray. 1999. *Teaching in America: The Slow Revolution*. Cambridge, MA: Harvard University Press.

Greene, M. 1978. *Landscapes of Learning*. New York: Teachers College Press.

Greene, M. 1988. *Dialectic of Freedom*. New York: Teachers College Press.

Grossman, P., S. Wineburg, and S. Woolworth. 2001. "Toward a Theory of Teacher Community." *Teachers College Record* 103:6: 942–1012.

Grumet, M. R. 1988. *Bitter Milk: Women and Teaching*. Amherst: University of Massachusetts Press.

Gutmann, A. 1999. *Democratic Education*. Princeton, NJ: Princeton University Press.

Harding, S. 1991. *Whose Science? Whose Knowledge?: Thinking from Women's Lives*. Ithaca, NY: Cornell University Press.

Hargreaves, A. 1991. "Contrived Collegiality: The Micropolitics of Teacher Collaboration." In *The Politics of Life in Schools*, ed. J. Blasé, 46–72. New York: Sage Publications.

Hargreaves, A. 1994. *Changing Teachers, Changing Times: Teachers' Work and Culture in the Postmodern Age*. New York: Teachers College Press.

Hofmann, N. 1981. *Woman's True Profession: Voices from the History of Teaching*. New York: Feminist Press.

Hord, S. M. 2004. *Learning Together, Leading Together: Changing Schools through Professional Learning Communities*. New York: Teachers College Press

Kegan, R. 1983. *The Evolving Self*. Cambridge, MA: Harvard University Press.

Kegan, R. 2002. *How the Way We Talk Can Change the Way We Work: Seven Languages for Transformation*. San Francisco: Jossey-Bass.

Lave, J., and E. Wenger. 1991. *Situated Learning: Legitimate Peripheral Participation*. New York: Cambridge University Press.

Lieberman, A., and D. R. Wood. 2002. *Inside the National Writing Project: Connecting Network Learning and Classroom Teaching*. New York: Teachers College Press.

Little, J. W. 1990. "The Persistence of Privacy: Autonomy and Initiative in Teachers' Professional Relations." *Teachers College Record* 91:4: 509–36.

Little, J. W. 2002. "Professional Community and the Problem of High School Reform." *International Journal of Educational Research* 37: 693–714.

Lortie, D. 1975. *Schoolteacher: A Sociological Study*. Chicago, IL: University of Chicago Press.

Martin, J. R. 1994. *Changing the Educational Landscape*. New York: Routledge.

McDonald, J. P., N. Mohr, A. Dichter, and E. C. McDonald. 2003. *The Power of Protocols: An Educator's Guide to Better Practice*. New York: Teachers College Press.

McLaughlin, M. W., and J. E. Talbert. 2001. *Professional Communities and the Work of High School Teaching*. Chicago, IL: University of Chicago Press.

Mead, G. H. 1967. *Mind, Self and Society: From a Social Behaviorist Perspective*. Chicago, IL: University of Chicago Press.

Meier, D. 1995. *The Power of Their Ideas*. Boston, MA: Beacon Press.

Mezirow, J., and associates. 2000. *Learning as Transformation: Critical Perspectives on a Theory in Progress*. San Francisco: Jossey-Bass.

Miller, J. B. 1986. *Toward a New Psychology of Women*. 2nd ed. Boston, MA: Beacon Press.

Oakes, J., K. H. Quartz, S. Ryan, and M. Lipton. 2000. *Becoming Good American Schools: The Struggle for Civic Virtue in Education Reform*. San Francisco: Jossey-Bass.

Piaget, J. 2001. *Psychology of Intelligence*. New York: Routledge.

Potter, K. 2004. *Pathways to Change: Collaboration and Inquiry*. Unpublished paper for the American Educational Research Association Annual Conference, San Diego, CA.

Power, M. 1997. *The Audit Society: Rituals of Verification*. New York: Oxford University Press.

Reinhart, J. 2004. *Lancaster Learning Communities: A Journey*. Unpublished paper for the American Educational Research Association Annual Conference, San Diego, CA.

Sarason, S. B. 1991. *The Predictable Failure of Educational Reform*. San Francisco, CA: Jossey-Bass.

Sarason, S. B. 1996. *Revisiting the Culture of the School and the Problem of Change*. New York: Teachers College Press.

Schaefer, R. J. 1967. *The School as Center of Inquiry*. New York: Harper & Row.

Schon, D. A. 1983. *The Reflective Practitioner*. New York: Basic Books.

Scott, A. O. 2003 (February 9). "Destined for Failure." *New York Times Magazine*, 15.

Senge, P., N. Cambron-McCabe, T. Lucas, B. Smith, J. Dutton, and A. Kleiner. 2000. *Schools that Learn: A Fifth Discipline Fieldbook for Educators, Parents, and Everyone Who Cares about Education*. New York: Doubleday Dell.

Sockett, H. 1993. *The Moral Base for Teacher Professionalism*. New York: Teachers College Press.

Taylor, C. 1992. *The Sources of the Self: The Making of the Modern Identity*. Cambridge, MA: Harvard University Press.

Tyack, D. B. 1974. *The One Best System: A History of American Urban Education*. Cambridge, MA: Harvard University Press.

Vygotsky, L. 1978. *Mind in Society*. Cambridge, MA: Harvard University Press.

Vygotsky, L. 1986. *Thought and Language*. Cambridge, MA: MIT Press.

Waller, W. 1967 [1932]. *The Sociology of Teaching*. New York: Wiley.

Weinbaum, A., D. Allen, and T. Blythe. 2004. *The Power of Protocols*. New York: Teachers College Press.

Wenger, E. 1998. *Communities of Practice: Learning, Meaning, and Identity*. Cambridge: Cambridge University Press.

Wessler, S. L. 2003. *The Respectful School: How Educators and Students Can Conquer Hate and Harassment*. Alexandria, VA: Association for Supervision and Curriculum Development.

Westheimer, J. 1998. *Among Schoolteachers: Community, Autonomy, and Ideology in Teachers' Work*. New York: Teachers College Press.

Wood, D. R. 2007. "Teachers' Learning Communities: Catalyst for Change or Infrastructure for the Status Quo?" *Teachers College Record* 109:3: 699–739.

Wood, D. R., and A. Lieberman. 2000. "Teachers as Authors: The National Writing Project's Approach to Professional Development." In *Escapes from High Theory: Theory-Assisted Practice*, special ed. of *International Journal of Leadership in Education 3:3*, ed. C. A. Mullen and J. S. Kaminsky, 255–73.

∽ 4 ଚ∾

LEARNING COMMUNITIES IN AN ERA OF HIGH-STAKES ACCOUNTABILITY

DIANE YENDOL-HOPPEY

When the federal legislation known as No Child Left Behind became law in 2001, Florida school systems were already grappling with the state-mandated A-Plus Accountability Program enacted in 2000. As was true in many other states, Florida's "A-Plus" legislation was intended as an educational improvement program that would measure school effectiveness through a standardized test: the Florida Comprehensive Assessment Test (FCAT). A central feature of the policy as it was enacted was that it linked students' test scores to school funding and pupil advancement; grades of A, B, C, D, and F were assigned to schools based on the test scores.

In the years since A-Plus and NCLB became law, these policies have reshaped the work of Florida's educators. For example, as a result of FCAT, many Florida teachers have increasingly relied on highly prescriptive lecture, question-and-answer formats, and FCAT worksheets, thereby creating a narrowed curriculum emphasizing basic mathematics and reading. The pressure to raise test scores also created a new emphasis on ability grouping, despite decades of evidence suggesting its ineffectiveness.

According to George (2001), these policies have created some unintended effects, including driving away many of Florida's best teachers, as the definition of school success grew exceedingly narrow. In addition, the accountability pressures have dramatically diminished teachers' ownership, control, and responsibility for their own professional development in favor of close, directed attention to the tested curriculum.

Leaders of Florida school systems have responded to the accountability policies in varied ways. In some school systems, a mandated curriculum now emphasizes preparing students for the state test. A few school districts recognized the short-sightedness of a mandated curriculum and the importance of authentically engaging teachers in developing a response to these accountability challenges. Still other systems tried to do both—mandating curriculum while at the same time encouraging teachers to collaborate in order to better understand how to meet each student's unique needs.

In an effort to help Florida's educators cope with the resultant tensions, the state initiated an additional policy that called for the implementation of professional learning communities in schools as a tool for teacher development and involvement in the context of increased accountability. This new policy, drawing on Hord (2004), describes the professional learning community (PLC) as a collegial group of educators united in its commitment to student learning, to sharing a vision, to working and learning collaboratively, to visiting and reviewing other classrooms, and to participating in decision making. According to Hord (2004), the benefits of PLCs include the reduced isolation of teachers, better-informed and more committed teachers, and academic gains for students. Hord notes, "As an organizational arrangement, the professional learning community is seen as a powerful staff-development approach and a potent strategy for school change and improvement" (27).

Florida's high-stakes accountability policies, coupled with the push for creating professional learning communities, have set up conflicting expectations for schools. On the one hand, the high-stakes approach encourages a curriculum aligned with the test, which puts teachers in the position of teaching what will be tested—a role that simply enacts decisions made elsewhere. The PLC approach assumes that teachers need to make decisions collaboratively, taking advantage of their professional judgments and decision making. One result has been that Florida educators have experienced tensions as these two initiatives collide.

This chapter identifies and illustrates three lessons gleaned from the realities of how a learning community initiative is likely to collide with high-stakes accountability, and the impact of such a collision on teacher and student learning. It draws on four years of documentation in the Beach County Public School System, as educators there participated in the Peer Collaboration Initiative funded by the Lucent Technologies Foundation. Beach County's experiences with Lucent Learning Communities (LLCs) demonstrate how accountability pressures influenced the work in that initiative.

THE PEER COLLABORATION INITIATIVE IN BEACH COUNTY

With more than 260,000 students in more than 200 schools, the Beach County Public School System (BCPSS) is one of the largest school systems in the United States. As one of the nation's fastest-growing districts, it serves a unique combination of urban and suburban students. Students represent more than 150 countries and speak fifty-seven languages. Faced with a vast array of challenges in meeting the diverse needs of its students, the school system is a huge, highly bureaucratic, organizational structure.

During the period of time described in this chapter, most Beach County educators felt tremendous pressure to teach the FCAT content, which in turn significantly influenced both curriculum and instructional decision making. The teachers described the test as "hanging over their heads," and the influence of the test results on the future of Beach County teachers and their students made the FCAT a high-stress test that affected morale in every school. One teacher explains:

> Morale has gone down more this year because of the FCAT. There is more stress and anxiety. FCAT makes good teachers feel that they are not worthy. I think that the whole accountability push is to get rid of bad teachers. Unfortunately, it is having the opposite effect.

Several teachers spoke of how test-related stress affected them, their teaching, and their students. As one teacher related:

> I was one of those people who became very stressed by [FCAT]. I think I sacrificed some of the creativity and warmth that I would have used; I got very business-like, and I may have made some of the kids stressed and tense. (Interview, 2001)

The intense pressures indicated in the aforementioned quotes set the stage for understanding the complexity that high-stakes accountability imposes on the LLC work.

This LLC work began with one of the district's subunits, called a zone, within the BCPSS. The smallest of the district's zones, it comprised a high school, a middle school, and three feeder elementary schools. This

zone was selected, in part, because of its size and a history of involvement with the Coalition of Essential Schools (CES) (CES 2005), a reform
initiative consistent with many of the LLCs' conceptual underpinnings.

During the first year in the Peer Collaboration Initiative, each of the
five participating schools established one or more LLCs consisting of
ten to fifteen voluntary members per group. These groups met from one
to three hours each month throughout the school year. During years
two and three, the number of LLCs expanded within each school; by
the end of year three, each of the five schools claimed 90 to 100 percent
participation. Also by year three, only 36 percent of the LLC participants defined their monthly participation as mandated, most of the
LLCs possessed a consistent internal coach, and membership in the various groups remained steady.

Consistent with the initiative's design (as described in chapter 2),
the LLC internal coaches were school-based volunteers trained by external National School Reform Faculty (NSRF) coaches with experience in
engaging professional educators in dialogue and reflection. As the external coach gradually withdrew from his role with Beach County, the
pool of trained internal coaches expanded to include new coaches each
year. Eventually, the external coach intentionally "worked his way out
of a job" and was replaced by a Beach County professional development specialist who became LLC director. She then worked directly
with school-based internal coaches and principals to implant the work
more deeply and organically into the Beach County system.

Upon completion of the first three years of the Lucent-funded LLC
work, the Beach County Human Resource Department (HRD) began
disseminating the LLC work to other zones within the school district.
This local effort was timely, paralleling the new statewide initiative
mandating professional learning communities as part of the state's call
for job-embedded professional development, as illustrated by the following statement from the Florida Department of Education:

> Learning communities are small groups of faculty who meet
> regularly to study more effective learning and teaching prac-
> tices. These groups are considered learning communities if they
> identify new programs or topics to investigate, gather research
> and studies on new approaches, and share their findings, or
> implement and study the effectiveness of new practices and
> share these results with other faculty in the school.

The movement to other zones in the district began with the development of schools that the HRD coordinator considered "ready" for LLC

work. These conditions of readiness included (1) a principal who understands and supports job-embedded professional development, (2) schools with a critical mass of teachers displaying an interest in participating, and (3) schools with an identified area of need.

The initial LLC work in Beach County sought to adopt the NSRF structures, emphasizing Critical Friends Groups (CFGs 2005) and then shaping them to the needs of teachers within the local context. These learning communities were initially defined as small groups of educators within a participating school that were collaboratively involved in improving their teaching practices. Early in the development effort, one teacher described LLC work as

> people coming together, helping each other with their work by listening and presenting their perspectives. To make this possible, members have learned procedures to keep dialogue nonjudgmental and respectful. The premise is that two heads are better than one in generating self-improvement.

Another noted the following:

> An LLC is a forum for teachers and administrators to meet where the walls of isolation that are so prevalent in most schools are broken down. It allows the sharing of ideas and support for common work and goals.

These reflections represented the initial perceptions of a critical mass of teachers early in the LLC work.

Although creating a collaborative and safe culture was essential to building a foundation for the LLC work, these excerpts also indicate an interest on the part of teachers in deepening their own learning. Recognizing that teachers needed a shared focus and a set of shared tools in order for systematic study to occur, the documentation team (as explained in chapter 2) introduced collaborative inquiry as a unifying component for LLC work. Collaborative inquiry required the LLCs to engage in systematic and intentional study of a shared question using an inquiry cycle (Cochran-Smith and Lytle 1993; Dana and Yendol-Silva 2003). During this phase of LLC development, the groups sought to integrate the NSRF tools for creating safe and trusting communities, examining student work, and discussing dilemmas with the work of collaborative inquiry. As a result, the reshaped LLCs began by defining a shared purpose, establishing a common inquiry question, and then using the NSRF tools to support the collaborative pursuit of the inquiry.

Using data from the documentation of Beach County's four-year journey toward collaborative inquiry and an analysis with the LLC leadership about both successful and unsuccessful LLC efforts, three key lessons emerged about collaborative inquiry in the midst of high-stakes accountability. The themes of these lessons are building a shared understanding of LLC work, honoring the complexity of the inquiry process, and the elusive nature of changes in student learning

The following analysis of each lesson also provides insights into how teacher ownership, control, and responsibility are influenced by high-stakes accountability mandates.

LESSON 1: BUILDING A SHARED UNDERSTANDING OF LLC WORK

While various LLC leaders in Beach County consistently described the goal of LLCs as improving student learning through teacher learning, the LLC participants struggled to create a shared understanding of the type of work that should be done within the individual groups. Initially, learning community activity varied widely across the schools; for example, some middle schools used learning communities to plan middle school events to reward student behavior, while other groups collaboratively examined student work to enhance writing instruction. Some LLCs continually missed attending to the "learning component" that was the distinguishing quality of the LLC work by focusing primarily on decision-making activities or logistics. The lack of discrimination among these various kinds of activities led to confusion about what LLCs should be doing. Some LLCs continually neglected the focus on learning that was intended to be the distinguishing quality of LLC activity.

Upon recognizing the need for more clarity about the activities that comprise LLC work, the LLC members began to differentiate committees from learning communities. According to their analysis, the work of "committees" was focused on decision making. The work of "learning communities" was guided by an inquiry or a dilemma that led to an ongoing, reflection-oriented, collaborative effort to change teacher practice and student learning. In short, learning communities explicitly and intentionally fostered teacher learning.

Once the importance of making a distinction between the work of committees and learning communities was clear to the coaches, an essential part of the professional development offered to new principals, coaches, and participants became understanding the importance of identifying a specific teacher learning goal that would guide their LLC activity. In addition, the importance of guarding against professional learning community meetings being usurped for committee work also became a key component of leadership development efforts.

In schools where LLCs did not become mere committees, the LLCs often worked initially toward creating a safe environment and enhancing teacher morale. Those dual goals were a necessary first step in the group's movement toward collaborative teacher learning. Creating a safe environment focused on building trust and attended to the teachers' voiced need for safety and support as they worked under intense accountability pressures. This trust and support provided what the teachers explained was the necessary foundation for them to move away from isolation and toward collaboration within the professional learning communities. As one teacher said:

> I hope that people don't think that our talk can just be professional because we are meeting in LLCs. We have a lot going on as far as pressure in the schools. Teachers are exhausted and afraid in a lot of ways. Collaboration means we have to move beyond our fears and make time for working with others. It will take us some time to make this happen.

Thus teacher collaboration was an essential underpinning for the professional dialogue needed to influence teacher learning. However, teacher collaboration required the teachers to trust each other and to begin to feel hopeful that dedicating time to working together would improve their professional lives.

Those LLCs that had already established a climate of trust and safety spent much of their meeting time focused on morale boosting. In most cases, LLC participants indicated that the intensity and stress associated with the current high-stakes testing movement in Florida substantially lowered morale and placed teachers in a survival mode. The LLCs served a central role in countering low morale. By sharing with each other, teachers began to see that they were not alone in their feelings and reactions to the greatly altered instructional climate. They also recognized that they were stronger working together than they were working alone.

The LLC work that focused on improving morale and enhancing teachers' feelings of safety was an essential part of enhancing teacher job satisfaction. However, focusing solely on these types of activities left many teachers and administrators wondering how this collaborative, time-intensive work could move beyond "feel-good stuff" to more deeply influence teacher and student learning. As a result, in the more-developed LLCs, the work shifted toward cultivating professional dialogue around student work, dilemmas of practice, and teacher knowledge construction using protocols (NSRF 2005).

For example, an LLC coach might ask a teacher to present student work from her elementary math students using a "Looking at Student Work" protocol. When protocols began to guide teachers' work, professional conversations related to both teaching and learning became an outcome of their work together. Although this effort began to successfully shift the dialogue toward teacher professional learning, the protocols brought to the discussion a series of disconnected "aha" moments or insights. These discussions demonstrated a shift away from committee work to professional dialogue around issues of teaching and learning, but the protocols did not create a shared inquiry around which the group could rally. Instead, the group dialogue often moved from one topic to another without making connections to a broader, shared line of inquiry. For example, a group might discuss how a piece of student work could have been strengthened by using a rubric in the first half of the gathering and then shift to a discussion of how a prompt for student writing might have been differentiated to obtain a better writing sample. These two unrelated professional dialogues may have strengthened each presenting teacher's understanding; however, the dialogues were disconnected and rarely included follow-up, thus the meetings tended to move from one dilemma to another. As a result, the LLC groups sometimes lost energy, focus, and continuity—both between meetings and throughout the school year. One LLC leader shared the following:

> I know my group members really enjoy getting together and having the support of our LLC. This support is critical given the pressures we are experiencing in the school. Using the protocols, we have been able to use that context of support to change what we talk about when we meet and how we talk to each other. What seems to be missing is the link between meetings. Each meeting we talk about dilemmas or student work, but the focus is more on the individual teacher solving her dilemma rather than the group level. How does each member's work connect from one meeting to the next? How does our work connect to each other? As a coach, this makes it hard to think about what the work looks like over a longer period. It seems like after awhile, we had figured out the mechanics of the protocols but needed to move further.

In a variety of settings, the protocol activities often became an unsystematic piling up of events over time rather than a series of activities connected to a larger shared thread or theme.

As described in chapter 2, midway through the Lucent funding, Beach County educators and the external Lucent support team began to discuss how the LLCs could move beyond merely supporting individual teachers' reflections related to specific teaching practices to creating a critical mass of teachers who could collaboratively address the needs of students in their school. This movement toward identifying and promoting a shared purpose that would have the power to unite the participants of each LLC allowed collaborative inquiry to become the vehicle for focusing more explicitly on teacher and student learning.

For example, one school committed to improving reading instruction focused each of its five learning communities on a different aspect of reading instruction (vocabulary development, for example). Within each learning community, educators explored research related to the identified area, engaged in the examination of student work, and shared teaching dilemmas. Each of these activities was targeted on a shared guiding question, and teachers were encouraged to bring related student data to the meetings. These LLCs reflected the most sophisticated level of activity; they had moved from establishing trust and safety, through a variety of intermediary phases, to defining a shared inquiry that guided their dialogue.

As indicated, the activities of the LLCs early in the initiative varied substantially from one another, ranging from creating a trusting context, to enhancing morale, to differentiating learning communities from committee meetings, to focusing on individual teacher learning, to using specific protocols. The type of activity that each LLC engaged in depended on a number of factors, including the coach's understanding of what LLCs were to be about, the group's readiness and needs, and the school context. As a result, the timing of and emphasis on particular activities also varied across LLC groups. One coach new to the LLC work described the group's work in this way:

> At my school there is little morale, trust, and support. We have had to work on all these. The principal didn't really understand that learning communities are not committee meetings. She likes to take time from the meetings for other purposes. I am not sure the teachers in my group see how the reflections generated by the protocols are really going to help them respond to the pressure they are feeling from the principal and the county team that actually inspects the low-performing schools to improve student learning on the state test.

The previous example illustrates the complexity and confusions characteristic of early LLC work in Beach County. Given that a wide range of activities were at some point considered "the LLC work," participants and coaches often lost sight of the collaborative learning goal. Recognizing the need for clarification, the Beach County coordinator for the initiative regrouped by bringing the coaches together during the third year of the project. As a group, the coaches collaboratively redefined LLCs as "a group of educators that collaborate in a way that is sufficiently powerful to produce change in both educator practice and student learning." This definition provided the coaches with an ongoing reminder that LLC work is consonant with improving both teacher and student learning. After this point, the coaches began to gain understanding about how the LLCs could help them focus on student learning within a context of accountability. As the coaches increasingly allowed this definition of LLCs to guide their work, the teachers also became more aware of the purpose. The Beach County journey toward constructing a shared definition of collaborative work helped set the LLCs apart from committee work and clarified the unique "learning" goal of LLCs for future participants.

This lesson highlights how Beach County educators struggled over time with what their LLCs should be doing. Along the way, high-stakes accountability became a hindrance as well as a motivator to engage in collaborative teacher learning, for at least the following three reasons:

1. Because of the pressures of accountability, trust and safety among teachers had diminished, along with teacher morale. Participants in the early stages of LLCs in Beach County spent a tremendous amount of their time together reestablishing a more positive interpersonal culture using the strategies the coaches had learned from the NSRF trainings.

2. The demands of accountability had shifted teacher professional development away from teacher-driven learning toward compliance with externally made decisions, particularly within low-scoring schools. Prior to the onset of accountability pressures, Beach County had lacked the structural and cultural components, such as school-based decision making and teacher leadership, which could facilitate teacher ownership of their professional growth. As a result, LLC movement in that direction was an enormous task that called for powerful shifts in the way professional development was conceived and enacted. While this shift was the explicit goal of the designers of the Peer Collaboration Initiative, recognition by Beach County LLC leaders of just how daunting the work would be took a while to develop.

3. Again prompted by the demands of high-stakes accountability, the coaches and district leaders felt pressed to make the LLC work and its ties to student learning explicit. During the third year, a subset of the

LLCs that was able to move beyond the initial phases of defining its work began to create opportunities for collaborative professional learning that could result in teacher and student learning focused on a shared question related to its school's needs. Its work would mirror the process of teacher inquiry, defined by Cochran-Smith and Lytle (1993) as systematic and intentional study. The inquiry process offered some of the LLCs a focus for their shared work. Unfortunately, due to the degenerated school culture and the lack of structures that would support job-embedded professional development, high-stakes accountability significantly hindered the movement of many LLCs toward teacher ownership of their professional growth. Once a shared focus was identified, however, accountability served to motivate the teachers to work on connecting student and teacher learning.

LESSON 2: HONORING THE COMPLEXITY OF THE INQUIRY PROCESS

As a result of the LLC director's effort to emphasize learning community work as "sufficiently powerful enough to produce change in both educator practice and student learning," during the third year some of the groups were able to move toward shared inquiry focused on needs that had been brought to light by accountability data. For example, some groups explored how to address the needs of the low-achieving readers in their schools. By collaboratively focusing on a particular student learning need identified as collectively important to the LLC members, the members began both to reclaim ownership of their professional growth and to document the impact of their work on teacher and student learning. The pressure of accountability motivated the LLCs not only to focus on teacher and student learning but also to document that learning for others to see.

Although shared inquiry became the vehicle for teacher collaboration within a subset of the LLCs, several other factors also influenced the success of those groups. These factors included the process used, the participants, and the size/focus of the question that guided their work. Often these three factors—separately or in combination—inhibited or limited an LLC's progress.

The first factor that became problematic was truly understanding the process of collaborative inquiry. Due to the high-stakes context, developing such an understanding proved challenging for many groups. The process required moving beyond identifying a question to developing a plan, collecting multiple types of data, and analyzing the data.

Given that this inquiry process was new to the teachers and coaches, many of the LLC coaches struggled with moving their learning communities beyond establishing trust and safety. They found it difficult to help teachers begin to embrace responsibility for their own professional learning. At the root of this difficulty was the passive disposition toward professional learning created by the district's practice of bombarding teachers with "trainings" that bore little relation to their daily work in the classroom.

Although many of the LLC groups never reached the stage of establishing a focus on shared inquiry, the groups that did identify a shared focus struggled to understand the type of data that might be collected that could move teachers beyond framing a question relating to high-stakes data or engaging in an inquiry that relied on data from high-stakes tests. The coaches and the LLC members had difficulty moving beyond questions that directly related to high-stakes testing or that used multiple types of data.

The LLC coaches realized that understanding the proper work of learning communities and the process of inquiry were necessary but not sufficient conditions for facilitating or coaching the entire process. They saw the need to establish a strong coaching regimen that could not only create a context for professional sharing but also the context for shared inquiry focused on teachers' reclaiming responsibility for their professional learning. As a result, the LLC coaches met regularly to explore and refine their understanding of the inquiry process, with the goal of providing greater clarity about the kinds of LLC activities that would lead to deliberate changes in classroom practice and documented changes in student learning. One coach observed this:

> We have learned about a lot of tools that can change the nature of our conversations. However, I am not yet sure how to integrate these tools into the inquiry process. They often feel separate, and an even bigger barrier is that there are competing accountability needs that trump teacher time and run counter or separate to the LLC work.

This comment highlights the tensions that LLC coaches and teachers felt related to the inquiry process; these tensions complicated movement toward collaborative inquiry.

Beyond the fact that the process mattered, *participants* mattered. Essential components of an effective LLC were a supportive principal, a strong coach, LLC members who were interested in job-embedded professional development, and an external critical friend. Without these elements, the LLC work often never reached the goal of collaborative inquiry, lost focus, or failed to make timely progress.

The principal's knowledge and understanding of the meaning of LLC work proved essential. Without this understanding, principals often asked LLCs to engage in committee work or failed to provide adequate time for LLC collaboration. One coach remarked: "When the principal is writing checks during your learning community meeting instead of being present and engaged, you know they don't get the work and their role in the work." Another coach explained: "My principal wants to continually give us work to do at the LLC meetings, and I am constantly reminding her that we need to protect this time for teacher learning tasks." Thus the principal played a key role in all the LLC work, even when he or she was not an LLC participant.

In addition, the internal coach needed to have a clear understanding of the LLC work as well as to be skilled in both facilitation and organization. The district LLC director observed the following:

Coaches vary in their understanding of the work and ability to keep their group moving forward. It is hard for the coaches to lead collaborative inquiry work before they have really gained an idea of the process for themselves. We are at all different levels.

The motivation and interest level of the LLC participants were equally important. One coach said this:

Some of my group members are really leading the work. They volunteer to take on leadership roles within the group and seem to really feel passionate for the work. One of the teachers in my group actually shows this deep passion for the writing curriculum work, while I have a few others that seem like they just show up for the meeting. I am not sure how to get buy-in from those people.

When participants understood the LLC work, felt passionately about the shared question, and displayed a positive disposition toward job-embedded learning, the LLC group thrived. When groups did not possess these characteristics, their work typically wandered.

Finally, external pressure from those outside of the district provoked growth within the individual LLCs. Initially this external pressure came from the external coach. He commented:

I know my job is to help them get started and to think more deeply about how they can work together. I find myself asking clarifying and probing questions to help the coaches and LLC participants to uncover important questions about the way they work together. My goal is to eventually leave them with the skills to engage in this work and to work my way out of the job.

However, once the external coach removed himself from direct interaction with the individual LLCs, the pressure typically came from the LLC director or the outside documenter. The LLC director noted:

The pressure that I provide sets targets or benchmarks for their work. By a certain meeting they bring a question, at another meeting they bring data. . . . I also rely on external pressure to keep me on track. They are always asking me questions about our work and reminding me of things that need to be attended to. We problem solve together. Otherwise, I can get lost in the details.

To a large degree, the ability of a group to effectively engage in collaborative inquiry relied on a skilled facilitator who was able to set benchmarks and work with critical friends to create the right conditions or process for professional learning. This was particularly important due to the work intensity generated by accountability demands.

In addition to understanding the process and engaging the participants, the size and the focus of the inquiry question influenced an LLC's ability to address accountability-related dilemmas. As internal coaching became more sophisticated, substantial efforts were made to help LLCs generate questions. These efforts centered on helping the group focus on a question that was within their sphere of influence, represented a shared interest, and focused on student learning needs. For example, once a group moved toward collaborative inquiry, the questions to be explored originated from the high-stakes data rather than from instructional difficulties expressed by individual teachers. One coach shared the following:

Our school's reading scores really dropped last year, so we decided to make reading the focus of our LLC work this year: "How can we improve student reading at NE?" I am not sure how to organize our work, though, because there is so much to focus on in reading. It is too big.

With the help of the external documenter and the LLC director, some of the LLCs learned over time how to craft an inquiry question by making a distinction between broad questions, guiding questions, and narrow questions. The group usually began by crafting a broad question attached to a school improvement goal that was generated by high-stakes accountability data, such as "How can we improve reading?" Then it developed guiding questions that focused its work on a particular subarea of the larger topic. In the case of reading, one LLC decided to focus on vocabulary development; two other groups in the same school targeted fluency and comprehension, respectively. Finally, within the subarea, the teachers developed their own narrower questions that they committed themselves to studying throughout the year. For example, one teacher within the vocabulary group, Louise, decided to study student learning using the "word wall" strategy. She drew on Brabham and Villaume's work (2001), as described in the article "Building Walls of Words." Her inquiry questions were: "How can the word wall help my students develop vocabulary? And will they find meaning in the activity?" Louise explained:

> Since we were doing a genre study on fractured fairy tales, I decided to engage my students in a word hunt. As the students reread the story with their group, they identified any words they found particularly descriptive or new to them. They then put these words on a chart, and we integrated these words into the activities at the literacy centers. In terms of results, I did not notice a difference in my students who were already reading fluently. However, the struggling readers were beginning to point out words that they found were new to them and began breaking words apart with me during guided reading. It was as if they now had access to some knowledge about attacking new words that they did not have before.

As indicated in Louise's summary, the process of moving to a narrow question typically focused on implementing a new instructional strategy or curriculum tool and studying the students' learning. As teachers collaboratively struggled to state, study, and capture changes in teacher and student learning, their inquiry questions became more sophisticated. Although teachers began to use these three levels of questions to guide their collaborative and individual inquiry, the questions were driven by the accountability data, and the strategies had to be viable within the context of the many existing reading mandates. Thus the scope and focus of the inquiry was both facilitated and limited by accountability pressures.

In sum, as the participants in the Beach County LLCs fought to reclaim their responsibility for teacher and student learning, the importance of the process used, the participants, and the size/focus of the question became vitally important. As discussed earlier, many times LLCs did not move beyond safety, morale, protocols, and committee work to begin to enact changes in professional practice that could be captured in learning gains for students. The LLCs that reached a higher level of sophistication typically had facilitators who could create a strong understanding of the process, a school context that would support job-embedded professional learning, a culture that embraced teacher responsibility for professional learning, and a well-crafted question that could be systematically studied. These groups were able to develop a context for learning that honored the complexity of the inquiry process within a context of high-stakes accountability.

LESSON 3: THE ELUSIVE NATURE OF CHANGES IN STUDENT LEARNING

After four years of participation in the Peer Collaboration Initiative, teachers reported—on the survey and in interviews—a heightened sense of satisfaction with their own professional learning. The data also indicated that due to the job-embedded nature of the LLC work and the opportunity for teachers to engage in dialogue with each other about their teaching practices, participants viewed LLCs as a much more powerful form of professional development than district workshops. Specifically, in a report submitted to the Lucent Foundation (Yendol-Hoppey 2004), LLC participants identified LLCs as

> offering a new and enhanced opportunity to problem solve and implement change as a result of LLC participation. Respondents identified a heightened level of collaborative problem solving and innovation as a result of the LLCs.

Participants overwhelmingly indicated that they had indeed engaged in innovation and change within their classroom context as a result of the LLCs. Teachers acknowledged the changes in how they experienced professional development by describing a significant shift from a traditional workshop approach to staff development to a collaborative, job-embedded, inquiry-driven approach.

Although the shift toward job-embedded professional development is striking, enumerating specific changes in student learning related to LLC collaboration remained elusive, both to the LLC director and to the external documenters. Although the researchers were able to identify the existence of a subset of LLCs with a shared inquiry and a strong culture of professional learning, an adequate set of data was never identified that could explicitly account for changes in children's learning resulting specifically from teachers' participation in an LLC.

A number of barriers contributed to the lack of data on student learning. First, the identification of specific practices that changed as a result of LLC work was hampered by lack of documentation from one meeting to the next. Specific structures needed to be in place to chart what the teacher had learned during a particular LLC meeting, and how that new learning would be carried out in the classroom. Moreover, specific records would need to be maintained by the teacher that identified when new instruction took place and what was learned by reviewing the student work related to the instructional goal. These structures would require teachers to create an audit trail of their work that delineates the connection between new practice and student outcomes.

As explained in chapter 2, the leaders of the Peer Collaboration Initiative expected each member of an LLC to investigate a unique question about his or her practice. However, in the third year of the project, a set of LLCs in Beach County agreed to engage in collective inquiry as a strategy for both enhancing teaching and learning and documenting impact. This strategy, which was developed by a design team meeting in Maine in December 2002 (see chapter 2), enhanced participation in collective inquiry in Beach County beyond the pilot LLCs. Moreover, the added pressure of high-stakes accountability in Florida led teachers to focus on their students' test scores as the primary source of data for their inquiry.

The experience of these LLCs indicates that teachers needed a rich repertoire of assessment tools that could be used to document changes in student learning related to their inquiry. Just as researchers often struggle to identify instruments that capture the constructs central to their work, teachers also have difficulty identifying, modifying, and creating assessment tools able to measure specific changes in student learning that result from a specific instructional intervention. In addition, the complexity of student learning within any given classroom makes attributing learning to a specific innovation elusive. As accountability pressures increase, teachers are expected to prepare their students for yearly assessments of state standards, but these same teachers also need to develop a tool kit of traditional and alternative assessments to serve as formative guides to their planning.

Future LLC work will require more sophisticated coaching to help teachers create a plan that can capture changes in their own learning as well as document links to student learning. In order for teachers to have a professional role in responding proactively to the demands of accountability, they will need help, not only in further developing inquiry skills, but also in creating an audit trail that can capture the changes in their students' work. This audit trail adds an additional demand to an already overworked profession (Hargreaves 1994).

FINAL THOUGHTS

This four-year LLC journey captured the process used by Beach County educators in building LLCs that were focused on changing teacher practice, with the aim of promoting student learning, through collaborative inquiry within an LLC. When the Beach County educators began the work, no template existed to chart their course within an LLC, and the culture did not typically provide job-embedded, teacher-driven work.

At the outset of the LLC work, high-stakes accountability had created a context characterized by lack of trust and safety—one in which many Florida teachers were sent to "trainings" and provided with materials that resembled highly prescriptive lecture, question-and-answer formats, and FCAT worksheets. The accountability pressures had shifted the focus away from engaging curriculum to emphasizing the most basic courses in mathematics and reading. The Beach County work presents an example of how the LLCs began a movement away from the conditions created by accountability by devising spaces for dialogue around shared questions.

Given the challenge of doing this kind of work within an era of intense accountability, educators would benefit from the lessons learned by these educators. First, it is essential that LLC participants understand their purpose and that the building principal be willing to devote and protect teacher time for professional learning. Second, groups such as LLCs need skilled coaches who can help the groups be purposeful and intentional when crafting their own process, facilitating participants, and managing the complexity and focus of the inquiry question. This kind of teacher leadership role needs to be cultivated and supported. Third, teachers in such groups need support in identifying and developing the most effective tools for data collection and assessment.

Cultivating the LLCs as professional learning communities required a dramatic shift in the professional culture of most of the Beach County schools—moving the responsibility for professional learning closer to the teachers, with student learning as the goal. This "reculturing" required dramatic changes in those rituals, roles, and responsibilities that take time, commitment, and specific knowledge on the part of the group members, coaches, and school leaders. As is often the case with other reform initiatives, after almost four years of work the Beach County participants described the LLCs as "just coming into their own" as vehicles for teacher learning. The LLCs were by no means "quick fixes" to a political problem, but they have shown considerable potential as "real fixes" to real problems of practice.

Given the challenges presented by high-stakes accountability, cultivating LLCs that have the potential for professional development that enhances student learning will take substantial time, resources, and commitment from those both inside and outside the learning community. And meaningful change requires pressure paired with support. In Florida, where accountability creates pressure and professional learning communities have been mandated to support teacher learning, the pairing of pressure and support could potentially create an opportunity for powerful teacher learning to occur. The lessons learned from Beach County acknowledge the sophistication that will be required of those who would support, lead, and participate in learning community work.

This study provides glimmers of hope to educators who believe that learning communities can serve as a motivating and uniting force that has the potential to initiate a swell of energy that can transform schools to places where all teachers and students are learning. First, however, it will be necessary for leaders at all levels—district, state, and national—to recognize the adverse influence that high-stakes accountability pressures can have on educators who are committed to improving learning through collaboration in professional learning communities. In recognizing these adverse influences, leaders must be prepared to provide adequate support for the educators who work most closely with our students.

REFERENCES

Brabham, E. G., and S. K. Villaume. 2001. "Building Walls of Words." *Reading Teacher* 54:7: 700–702.

Coalition of Essential Schools (CES). 2005. *The Common Principles: Elementary and Secondary School Inclusive*. Retrieved September 6, 2005, from http://www.essentialschools.org/pub/ces_docs/about/phil/10cps/10cps.html.

Cochran-Smith, M., and S. Lytle. 1993. *Inside Outside: Teacher Research and Knowledge*. New York: Teachers College Press.

Collaborative Inquiry and Development Group. 2005. Retrieved October 31, 2005, from http://www.usm.maine.edu/cid/.

Critical Friends Groups (CFGs). 2005. Retrieved October 31, 2005, from http://www.cesnorthwest.org/critical_friends_groups.htm.

Dana, N. F., and D. Yendol-Silva. 2003. *The Reflective Teacher's Guide to Action Research: Learning to Teach and Teaching to Learn through Classroom Inquiry*. Thousand Oaks, CA: Corwin Press.

Florida Department of Education. 2000. *Florida School Indicators Report*. http://www.info.doe.state.fl.us/fsir/.

George, P. 2001. "A+ Accountability in Florida?" *Educational Leadership* 59:1: 28–32.

Hargreaves, A. 1994. *Changing Teachers, Changing Times: Teachers' Work and Culture in the Postmodern Age*. New York: Teachers College Press.

Hord, S. M. 2004. *Learning Together, Leading Together: Changing Schools through Professional Learning Communities*. New York: Teachers College Press.

National School Reform Faculty (NSRF). 2005. *NSRF Resources: Protocols*. Retrieved March 26, 2005, from http://www.nsrfharmony. org/protocols.html.

U.S. Department of Education. 2002. *No Child Left Behind Act*. Retrieved January 19, 2005, from http://www.ed.gov/policy/elsec/ leg/esea02/index.html.

Yendol-Hoppey, D. 2004. *Report to the Lucent Foundation*.

✑ 5 ✑

CONTEXT AND
COLLABORATION

Growing the Work in New Jersey

DEBRA R. SMITH, DICK CORBETT,
AND BRUCE L. WILSON

This book opened with the declaration that teachers' professional learning communities offer one of the more promising prospects for improving schools. At the same time, it was acknowledged that there are few road maps for just how that might happen. This chapter relates the stories of three districts in New Jersey supported financially, developmentally, and conceptually by the Alcatel-Lucent Foundation to enhance learning prospects for all students in their care. In New Jersey, the groups were dubbed collaborative learning communities (CLCs) rather than LLCs.

"How can the lessons of the Peer Collaboration Initiative [PCI, an earlier Alcatel-Lucent-supported reform, described in chapters 1 and 2] inform the design of a new initiative in New Jersey?" was the question posed by Hallie Tamez of The Philanthropic Initiative on behalf of the foundation as she convened representatives of the documentation research team and the National School Reform Faculty (external facilitators for the PCI and the soon-to-be-designed CLC Initiative) in Boston late in 2003. The documentation team members had arrived with a summary of lessons and recommendations that served as the starting point for discussion (see chapter 2).

Out of this day of dialogue, and over the next weeks, a new design emerged. New Jersey districts that had demonstrated a degree of readiness and commitment would be invited to apply to participate in a planning year (the 2003–2004 school year). This would entail forming a leadership design team (LDT), comprised of people in different roles, from classroom teachers to central office staff, that would become a learning community, participating in an introductory residential institute during the summer, and then meeting three hours each month with a skilled outside facilitator over the course of the school year. The team then would turn its focus to developing a three-year plan for embedding and expanding learning communities in the context of their districts, considering existing culture, structures, and processes. The data from this chapter include experiences of the authors, who have followed the New Jersey districts through planning and three years of implementation.

The foundation also hoped that these districts would begin to form a regional network that would provide sustained collaborative learning opportunities and mutual support across districts. The design of the planning year offered an opportunity to examine whether and how the work with district teams in learning communities leads to a coherent understanding of how learning communities might be incorporated systemically in district change efforts. The plan incorporated both documentation by an external team of researchers[1] (i.e., the authors of this chapter) and internal documentation conducted by the learning communities themselves. All of this documentation was intended to contribute to the groups' learning and to the larger understanding of the learning communities' experiences. The focus of the documentation during the planning year was to explore the experiences of the learning communities, the role of the external facilitators, and how the experiences of the teams were reflected in their district plans. In subsequent years, the documentation team examined how the CLCs and their work developed, as well as how they influenced, and were affected by, their local contexts.

In addition to the monthly visits by the external coaches, support for districts' systemic incorporation of the CLCs into the fabric of daily life in schools took the form of (1) a cross-district leadership CLC that met several times each year of implementation, (2) continuing cross-district coaches' seminars, and (3) the development of a cadre of "lead facilitators," those who first apprenticed to the external facilitators and then began to assume leadership of the CLC support in their own districts, as well as planning and leading the cross-district seminars.

In the following sections we tell the New Jersey story, first by describing briefly the context of the three districts.[2] Then we use data from our observations of the process to describe a set of themes associated with planning and implementing the CLCs. During the planning year, an LDT in each of the districts engaged in five common activities in pursuing the development of a strategy for introducing CLCs into its system. Along the way, the groups also had several similar experiences and realizations that shaped their work. However, as the districts moved into the implementation and the spreading of CLC work throughout the districts, more variation arose. That variation is captured by both the range of arrangements for the work of CLCs and the varying impacts on participants and their organizations. We end the chapter with a challenge for CLCs if they are to uphold the promise claimed by many believers of collaborative learning communities as a viable school reform tool. That challenge involves the need to articulate the clear connections between changing adult work and the ultimate learning of students.

THE THREE DISTRICTS

Three districts have participated throughout the four years of the Alcatel-Lucent Foundation-funded initiative: two urban "Abbott" districts and one suburban district. (The Abbott designation is well known throughout the state as a label for thirty districts that serve low-income and low-achieving populations with limited resources. Protracted legal battles over many years eventually produced a state Supreme Court ruling that declared the education provided by these schools to be inadequate and unconstitutional, forcing the state to provide significant new fiscal and educational resources, including the implementation of a comprehensive set of programs and reforms that included standards-based practices.) The general context in these two urban districts, unlike their suburban neighbor, was for high-stakes pressure to increase performance with intensive accountability accompanying the increased revenues.

The three districts were all quite large (relative to many districts in the state), with enrollment ranging from just under 8,000 to more than 13,000 students, and staff sizes ranging from 700 to more than 1,000 (see Table 5.1). The demographics of the two urban districts reflected a predominant enrollment of students of color; however, even the suburban district had diverse ethnicity in its classrooms. The most striking difference between the urban and suburban districts was the level of financial disadvantage. Only a small percentage of students in the suburban district (less than 10 percent) qualified for free or reduced lunch, whereas the majority of students in both urban districts qualified. Not surprisingly, student performance was closely associated with the demographics; nearly all of the students in the suburban district (about 90 percent) had met or exceeded state-defined reading proficiency levels, while the urban district scores were lower.

At the time the initiative began, the schools in the two urban districts, as part of the Abbott decision, were expected to adopt a whole-school reform model. In District B, most of the schools chose a single model whereas in District C a range of models was adopted. But as the federal No Child Left Behind legislation increasingly influenced local policy and practice, efforts were made to look for more consistency in curricular and instructional approaches for reading and mathematics. As a result, District C moved away from multiple reform models. Indeed, by the last year of the initiative, the state Department of Education expected all of the Abbott districts to engage in a process of developing professional learning communities as a primary reform tool. The two urban districts in this initiative found themselves in the lead among their Abbott colleagues because of their CLC work. All of the districts have had some history with multiple reform initiatives, so the idea of change is not a foreign one. District A, for example, had a *nuanced* approach to teacher inquiry and had worked with systemic change models for several years. District C had a long history of teacher networks and involvement with multiple reform projects through partnerships with national and international groups.

The three districts worked with an external facilitator who assisted the LDT at an initial summer institute, a winter retreat, and monthly within-district meetings throughout the school year. At the summer institute, the design teams were introduced to each other, the coaches, and the project plan for the year, and they had their first experiences using protocols and structured processes for professional dialogue. The winter retreat provided an opportunity to reconnect and to share and deepen their experiences as learning communities. After this gathering, the teams shifted their focus to developing their plans for the next three years.

The diversity across the districts was not reflected in events, experiences, and realizations that occurred during the planning year, but it began to play a huge role as the CLCs started their collaborative work of implementing CLCs.

THEMES IN PLANNING FOR CLCS:
THE WORK OF LDTS IN YEAR ONE

Although the LDTs worked in geographically proximate school districts, each operated in circumstances that varied widely. Leadership

Table 5.1. *Descriptive Characteristics of the Three New Jersey Districts*

Characteristics	Suburban District A	Urban District B	Urban District C
Student Enrollment	13,180	7,692	12,430
Number of Schools	17	13	24
Number of Teachers	1,000	700	1,025
Student Reading Proficiency	89%	60%	46%
Student Demographics	41% Asian 8% AA 7% Hispanic 84 native languages 9% free lunch	69% AA 29% Hispanic 70% free lunch	67% AA 29% Hispanic 59% free lunch
Contextual Highlights	Strong community support for schools High student performance and postsecondary enrollment Increasingly diverse student population taught by predominantly Caucasian staff History of teacher inquiry Change in superintendent, assistant superintendent, and curriculum director/project coordinator at end of planning year	All but two schools adopted "America's Choice" as their whole-school reform model. Mission-driven focus on providing an equitable education to all students Superintendent had a history of using teacher groups (critical friends groups) as a reform process. Change in curriculum director/project coordinator at end of planning year, year 1 and year 3	Schools adopted five or six different whole-school reform models but recently moved to uniform approaches to literacy and numeracy. Multiple role groups involved in reform History of teacher reform networks Schedule accommodates common planning time Change in project coordinator each year Change in superintendent and assistant superintendents at end of year 2.

changes, increasingly diverse student populations, internal district politics, court-ordered interventions, the weight of customary patterns of
interaction across role groups, and the departure of LDT members—all
of these had the potential to gnaw away at the possibility of participants' experiencing collaborative success or, at the least, to cause the
LDTs to evolve in such idiosyncratic ways so as to make them hardly
recognizable as having a common reform bond. This did not happen,
however. Instead, the process of wrestling with how to collaborate
meaningfully and effectively with colleagues—with the goal of produc-
ing a plan to spread collaborative learning communities throughout
their districts—led participants down a similar path.

Notably, five common activities across the three districts dotted the
landscape of the planning year. First, each district identified a team of
approximately twelve staff members from diverse positions (from
teachers to central office administrators and, in one case, a member of
the support staff) who met, planned, learned, and reflected on what
they had done to prepare for the implementation of CLCs over the
next three years. This was accomplished during monthly meetings
under the tutelage of an external facilitator who provided strategies,
advice, and support.

Second, the districts all began with unclear expectations about
where this project might take them, encountered some turbulence in the
middle of the journey, and offered uniform praise at the end for the
growth they had accomplished during the year. The initial ambivalence
and uncertainty grew out of the newness of this approach to reform
(i.e., educators were no longer told what they should do, with a prescriptive formula looming over them) and the guidance of outside
coaches, who insisted that answers would emerge from the collaborative endeavors of the participants. Remarkably, participants were willing to "hang in there" as the purpose began to grow clearer. But this
cooperative spirit did not minimize the fact that all of the districts
encountered significant challenges. Despite those challenges, the nearly
universal end-of-year assessment was upbeat. One group went so far as
to describe the year as "transformative," with members coming away
with a new set of skills on how to collaborate around teacher and
school improvement.

Third, all three district LDTs learned new "tools" (the language of
the participants) or "protocols" (the language of the external facilitators) as a way to interact, so everyone could share how they learned
from a text rendering, a consultancy, a tuning, a chalk talk, or connections as a way to structure constructive dialogue intended to improve
instruction and the quality of student work. Just learning to use these

tools competently was a big step in the right direction to prepare participants for the formation of CLCs across their districts. But the LDTs went beyond learning about these tools to starting to use them in their jobs. The protocols taught educators how to listen to each other more thoughtfully. For example, one district had had a particular policy in place for six months whose enforcement apparently was interpreted in multiple ways. By sharing ideas through the protocol process, the LDT at least reached a level of consensus about the meaning of the policy.

Fourth, from the onset of the initiative, the intention was that the districts would submit plans for the work of implementing CLCs at the end of the year. The request for proposals (RFP) asked the LDTs to first consider and capitalize on the naturally occurring opportunities for embedding CLCs in their district contexts, and then to identify how they would enhance their plan with additional foundation support. The drafting of proposals was expected, but what was not clear was how those plans would unfold. What emerged from the collaborative spirit of the learning throughout the year was an experience of shared ownership in the development of the proposals across the districts. Those who took part in the LDT work became the authors of the proposals. One district divided the LDT into subgroups, with different parts of the proposal parceled out to each. They then came together for collective review and worked toward consensus on the final proposal. In another district, each school was asked to respond to the RFP questions. One person then synthesized those perspectives; afterward, the larger LDT reviewed and revised the draft before submission. Underlying both of these examples was a very different way of operating relative to past practice and a feeling of real accomplishment by the team about this new approach.

Finally, the intention of the planning year was for the districts to incorporate documentation of the work as part of their ongoing activities. This grew out of some success in one district during the Peer Collaboration Initiative. The hope was that individual learning communities could document their own inquiry. But everyone struggled with what in theory sounded like a good idea but in practice never fully materialized. Challenges arose from technology glitches (i.e., the use of Web-based tools still in development), an unclear understanding of the purpose of the documentation and a lack of connection between the documentation and the work, and the challenge of deciding who would have access to the gathered information.

Throughout the year, doubts, misgivings, and frustrations arose, causing each team at some point to reflect on its purpose, role, and future. And then, for each, some event occurred that caused the team to recognize its own progress as a CLC and to rejuvenate expectations and commitment for promoting opportunities for others in the district to experience the same success. Evolving from these shared activities was the following set of five experiences and realizations that highlighted some valued aspect of the "work" that was central to making the planning year productive:

1. being exposed to high-quality external facilitation
2. understanding the meaning of "true" collaboration
3. achieving equity in collaborative adult relationships
4. taking advantage of "natural" connections
5. experiencing a "crystallizing" event

First, the LDT members attributed a number of benefits that accrued to *having external facilitators* involved in the process. The facilitators were responsible for initially enabling participants to build trust in one another; the facilitators held the group to using the protocols thoroughly; the facilitators kept the teams on track; the facilitators provided direct access to a storehouse of knowledge about collaboration and facilitating collaboration; and the facilitators leaped tall buildings in a single bound. And though various participants at one time or another wondered about the necessity of adhering rigidly to the protocols or about the deliberate pace of the first half of the year, they recognized by the end of the year that there was an underlying intentional logic to the process that now made sense to them.

Second, members of each LDT were amazed that they had worked with colleagues for so long and yet knew so little about *effective collaboration*. They also knew that educators forever had complained about how little time they had to interact with others, but that such precious time was still often squandered. The planning year therefore was not simply a case of discovering new labels to apply to actions at which they had been adept all along. Participants claimed that they had acquired knowledge and developed skills that they had never had before, both individually and collectively. Central to this burgeoning capacity was the realization that exploring one's professional practice with others was very likely the key to turning meetings into vehicles for improving student achievement.

Third, at the core of what made collaboration so valuable was the extent to which *equity was engendered* among participants. People talked about how much they had learned about other members' perspectives and how worthwhile it was to listen, really listen, to what people had to say and to feel that others were listening to them. This was a difficult process. Some LDTs struggled more than others in shedding the historical norms that had cloaked their interactions for years and repeatedly questioned whether the process would result in a new "look" in their districts. Eventually, however, it appeared that all three of the teams created a refreshing, trusting environment in which they explored, or at least began to explore, serious issues confronting their school systems.

Fourth, LDT members created *extensions of their LDT work* in their own professional settings. It was not clear to all whether they "should" be doing this, and some were extremely concerned that these initial experiences in classrooms, grade levels, schools, and the central office might in some way harm not only the rest of the planning year but also the future reception of CLCs as a central ingredient of reform. Nevertheless, the protocols and several CLCs did spread in "natural" ways as teachers tried out activities in their classrooms or grade-level meetings, principals (in conjunction with LDT teachers) invoked protocols for regularly scheduled faculty meetings or planning committees, and central office staff restructured existing committees and meetings on their work schedules. Thus LDT participants modeled more than proselytized collaboration and were nearly uniform in feeling that non-LDT staff who participated in these events left with a positive taste in their mouths.

Finally, despite considerable uncertainty about what might lie ahead for them, all of the teams noted that the Summer Institute was a startlingly effective time. Despite having only vague understandings about the role of the LDTs, participants had no uncertainty about having been introduced to new, effective ways of working with adults. This event, therefore, was universally acknowledged as a valuable and critical "send-off" for the coming year. Still, the LDTs experienced other "crystallizing events" that engendered a renewed commitment to the work and a hopeful outlook as proposal writing began. For one, it was an informal dinner at a conference when they constructed a protocol to use to discuss where they were as a team and what the team's role should be in the future (or if it even had one). For another, a staff development day in mid-March that the LDT planned and facilitated was sufficiently well received to cause the team to realize its incredible growth in knowledge and skill.

Each one of the above five experiences and realizations was equally important. Each team mutually reinforced one another as part of one gigantic feedback loop that occurred all year long. And, because the end of the planning year resulted in all of the teams committing to implement CLCs within their respective districts, the wisdom of giving LDTs a lengthy period of time in which to explore the meaning, problems, and prospects of CLCs would seem to be upheld. Problems arose, to be sure, but all appeared to be part and parcel of people constructing meaning out of their efforts to collaborate.

The LDTs essentially operated in rather "safe" environments. Their meetings and other activities put few strains on district resources. Even the natural opportunities upon which they seized to extend the protocols and CLC idea into the workplace required little initial commitment from non-LDT members. Either people encountered protocols in a meeting they were already going to attend, or they were "invited" to take part. In other words, the LDTs were not integrated into daily organizational routines in obtrusive, or even noticeable, ways. This afforded the LDTs, perhaps, a false sense of security about what would happen once CLCs sprouted from their plans.

THE IMPLEMENTATION PROCESS:
THE UNFOLDING OF CLCS ACROSS THE THREE DISTRICTS

Having a safe harbor from which to launch the CLCs was certainly not the situation the following year, when the time came to form actual CLCs in the schools. Unlike the planning year, the CLC operation collided head-on with particular contextual features in each district, which dramatically affected the arrangements for doing CLC "work" and the impact of that work. In this section we describe the variety of arrangements and summarize participants' assessments of those accommodations.

Arrangements for Doing "The Work"

The grant RFP anticipated that there would probably be some varied ways in which the districts were organized to do the work. That is exactly what happened. Most of these changes accommodated the special needs of individual districts, schools, or even CLCs. Here we describe the variety of arrangements and summarize participants' assessments of those accommodations.

The most obvious variety involved when and for how long CLC groups met to do their work. In the first year, the vast majority of CLCs met during the school day and devoted a two and a half hour block of time each month to the work. In the last two years, the coaches reported wider variation in meeting times. One district that provided released time during the school day in the first year opted not to follow that path the second year. Instead, teachers were asked to meet after school and were given a stipend for their time. Several meetings were able to take place during the school day—on district professional development days when teachers were working but students were absent. Those after-school meetings were usually two to two and a half hours in duration. Another district continued to meet during the school day and managed to find two and a half hour coverage for participants. The third district also met during the school day but could not find any large blocks of time. The longer time was replaced with more frequent, shorter blocks of time (thirty to forty-five minutes). Those blocks often represented teacher planning time or faculty meeting time. There was a near-unanimous consensus that trying to accomplish the work in shorter blocks of time or after school was not as productive as the school-day meetings. With shorter blocks of time it was often difficult to get into the "meat" of a protocol or to tackle an issue while also promoting time for "connections" or reflections. The after-school meetings did not have that challenge, but instead participants often ran out of energy after a busy day. Also, other demands invariably took precedence (child-care needs, other extracurricular assignments, or other faculty committee work) that caused participation to lag. One district promised staff that CLC meetings could substitute for attendance at faculty meetings; in practice, however, teachers ended up trying to juggle attendance at both. Even the times for shorter meetings during the school day were co-opted by administrators for other pressing issues. The bottom line was that the most productive time slots were extended blocks of time during the school day.

In the ideal world, when new ways of doing business or carrying out instructional practices are being introduced, it makes sense to match the coach-innovators with a partner. As the CLC initiative has matured, it has the added design feature of having trained a new group of coaches each year and expanded the knowledge base of more experienced coaches each year. In the ideal world it would be preferable for experienced and novice coaches to work alongside each other—not only in training but also in carrying out the work. In one district, monthly meetings with the external coaches were only made available to the novice coaches, whereas in the other two districts both novice and experienced coaches joined in. When facilitating CLC dialogue, coaches worked on their own as well as in pairs or triads. Even novice coaches took on the challenge of solo facilitation with CLCs. When coaches were paired up, there was not a consistent pattern of matching pairs— there were only experienced ones, only novice ones, and combined ones. In response to this variation, the common refrain from coaches was that "two heads are better than one." Those who had the opportunity to do so praised the experience of working alongside a peer. Invariably, people reported bringing different strengths, and it was always much easier to plan when "ideas could be bounced off of each other." That should not detract from the success of some solo coaches. Nevertheless, coaches collectively felt a higher comfort and success level when working with peers. One district accommodated that need for collegial planning by making sure that the coaches as a group met monthly—usually as an extension of the time with their external facilitator—to share ideas about what was and was not working.

During the first year of implementation, we noted that the preferred mode of working was to recruit volunteers. Indeed, some schools that started with mandatory participation backed away from the practice. That issue remains unresolved. The CLCs that made the most progress in terms of getting teachers to openly challenge their own and their peers' teaching practices were groups that volunteered and had built a strong level of trust through working together. But leaders of those same groups readily admitted that the challenge of making the changes to practice become part of the routine for all staff in the building (let alone the district) remained unsolved.

In schools or CLC groups where everyone was expected to participate, educators were also confronted with the reality that priorities other than CLC work often took precedence. So, while staff were told that this work was mandatory, they were also told that other work was more important. The mixed messages allowed this work to take a back seat. There appears to be no easy answer to this dilemma. What does become more evident as this work spreads across the three districts is that once participants get a taste of success in using protocols and structures for discussing adult and student work, they see the value in it. One suggestion, offered by a coach, was to start with a mandatory approach, providing everyone with an introduction and then moving to a gradual phasing in of the voluntary work. This approach, coupled with a healthy dose of support for the CLC work and a vision for the direction of that work, may be the boost that is needed to make it a part of the regular routine for all of the districts.

Whether the groups were voluntary or mandatory, they also varied in terms of group membership. In some CLCs it was dictated by who had common planning time (e.g., grade-level teams) or who had common subject-matter responsibility (math versus reading), or which group one normally affiliated with (new theme academies at several high schools), or a common role (subject-area supervisors, principals, technology facilitators), or with whom an available coach routinely provided other school improvement services (upper-grade English teachers), or more naturally evolving groups (a set of nontenured teachers). There was no clear pattern showing that any one type of group was more productive than another. What seemed to determine productivity was the extent to which the group could identify a mutually agreeable issue to address rather than a topic or topics they were told to work with. So, for example, a CLC of subject-area supervisors agreed to work together on a common process for confronting curriculum reform, and the nontenured teachers acknowledged their classroom challenges and built a process to share weaknesses and search for solutions together.

A variant on the coaching model adopted by one district was to bring experienced coaches to the table on a monthly basis with the external facilitator and plan for the training of a much broader group of second-level coaches spread throughout the district. Much of the time in the morning with the experienced coaches was spent planning activities for the second-level coaches that same afternoon. The expectation, then, was for those coaches to introduce the concepts underlying the Lucent work to a much wider base of teachers across the district. These second-level coaches are a group of support teachers provided to each building to promote improvement. A number of factors have prevented them from systematically using what they have learned in their buildings. First, their roles have been changing as the state redefines the shape of reform in Abbott districts. Second, building principals have the ultimate say in who will attend these meetings, so some principals send all of their support teachers (as many as three), and others send only one representative or, in some cases, none. Thus attendance is inconsistent, making it difficult to build a sustained understanding of the CLC work. Third, there is little accountability or follow-up that would permit, encourage, or require these educators to try out the ideas they have learned. The group reported that it felt like it was being asked to have teachers do one more thing when it was already overburdened with work. Group members did not feel as if they had ownership from the teachers with whom they work or the credibility to encourage teachers to try these ideas. Instead, they offered the ideas to teachers as something they might consider trying, but without the support to assist them in their efforts.

A final variation in arrangements was how the districts handled the composition of group membership when CLC work was continuing from the previous year. The majority of the groups were encouraged to keep the same members working together. That model seemed to work, with coaches offering the assessment that they were able to "hit the ground running." In some schools, however, the turnover was so great that it was impossible to maintain membership rolls. Those groups reportedly found it took much longer to get into the work. Likewise, some groups reported merging with another group, or in some cases having participants join for some sessions but not others. That latter experience was unproductive, with the CLC spending much of its precious time trying to bring new or part-time participants up to speed with both content and process. The blending of groups was a mixed bag. In some cases it brought new and energized people with different perspectives to the table, and in other cases it prompted new people to raise issues or test norms that had already been addressed by the group.

Participants pointed out a host of facilitative and inhibiting factors that influenced the operation of their CLCs, helping to cause this much wider divergence of experience from the planning year. Not surprisingly, *administrative support* was essential from both the central office and the building levels. Participants looked to the central office for signs that the CLC work was valued and integral to district plans. The key aspect of administrative support at the building level was securing and protecting the time that CLC participants had to take from their classrooms. *Competing demands for meeting time* emerged as a major struggle for coaches. This was especially true for CLCs that had been formed from preexisting groups (e.g., grade-level teams). Those groups often had other items on the agenda that trumped the CLC work. Another issue, according to coaches, was the *lack of clarity* about the direction of the work. Most agreed, after the fact, that it was essential to the development of trust and ownership not to be too prescriptive in the initial stages, and that, in most cases, vague expectations became a nonissue as the work progressed. In one district the *high turnover* in staff, even at the level of building and district leadership, meant that CLCs struggled with continuity, since participants' energies were directed at learning new or changing roles. A second district was also affected by staff turnover, with a different project coordinator each year and many of the coaches trained in the first two years having left the district by the third year. Finally, there was also a concern that the *time between meetings* was too long and allowed people to forget what they had taken away from previous meetings, which in turn made it difficult to easily establish an appropriate mind-set for current meetings.

INDIVIDUAL AND ORGANIZATIONAL IMPACTS

As has been described earlier in this chapter, people were enthusiastic about the opportunity to step out of the isolation of their classrooms and offices to come together for professional conversations with colleagues. They reported a variety of impacts on individuals and CLCs and, in some cases, impacts on students, the school climate, and the "way we do business."

All participants, of course, learned and used new protocols and processes for professional conversations. Many coaches reported that they had "added more tools to the toolbox," enhanced their facilitation skills, and boosted their confidence in guiding adult discussions. Moreover, they felt empowered and valued, as the following responses make clear:

> [It] makes me think differently about how to give information to a group. I am better able to help teachers when they are stuck.
>
> It empowered me; it heightened my awareness about facilitation of adult work. . . . I can see better what other teachers deal with. [I've] learned how to be quiet and delegate and focus on what the group needs.
>
> My work and training is valued. I feel more professional.
> [It's] nice to work with others who are willing to improve.

No matter what their professional role, many participants were more disposed to reflect about their work as a result of their CLC experiences. The meetings created a time and space that provided "the luxury of time to think—you have to figure out where you are to get where you want to go." In their daily work, administrators and teachers alike were more likely to pause and consider a situation before responding and to examine what they do in light of the needs of those with whom they work.

> Our CLC meeting is a retreat, a time to reflect. In my personal practice, it has helped me immensely. I am using technology more in my classes, and always looking for ways to have students do research initiatives and peer teach. . . . I am more proactive about finding ways for students to learn more actively, to engage their senses so they'll remember more.

In successful CLCs, the meetings themselves changed the way that adults communicated, solved problems, and worked together.

> It has changed the way that teachers talk to each other, it's changed the way that they look at group work when they're

together . . . the protocols lead to a nonjudgmental kind of way of looking at the work that we do with kids or the work that we do in school together as adults interacting.

Meetings are more effective, more focused. Once people see that, they recognize the value.

I've seen a big change in the way [people in my group] respond to things . . . in the way they approach difficult situations, they don't get flustered, they seek clarification . . . they can express themselves and work together better.

CLC members reported having better and deeper professional conversations and, in some cases, had taken action in their own classrooms and other settings. For example, in one CLC a teacher brought to the group a project she does every year for tuning, and she had much better results from students. Another reported that she had her students give each other feedback on their writing. As a result, their writing improved, and they felt more confident.

There were many examples of "on the cusp situations" in which CLCs had looked at student work, or were ready to look at work, but they did not actually take action because the year ended or something else disrupted their work:

In a district CLC that was examining student writing in relation to the state assessment: . . . people were shocked to realize that they had scored their students' work a "4" when the state had rated it as a "2." . . . We were figuring how to go deeper, but last month the meeting was cancelled, and this month will be the final meeting.

Another group looked at shared circles of work and then figured out a shared inquiry focus on mathematics. Unfortunately, the group did not continue to meet.

According to a third CLC that had had a difficult start: Once we got into student work, things got better, but now we're at the end of the year, and the time of day is taking the wind out of our sails. It has turned into an obligation rather than something we wanted to do.

A few CLCs had a deliberate, sustained focus on a particular aspect of students' learning. These groups were much more likely than others to examine closely student work and learning experiences and to make explicit connections to student learning, and they were able to report positive results. For example, in a CLC focused on embedding assessment in science, teachers tried things out in their classrooms, brought back student work, tuned their strategies, and went back to their classrooms again in a continuous cycle of inquiry.

A middle school CLC that focused on positive attitudes toward learning carried out collaborative action research. After reading some of the relevant literature, it shifted its own attitudes, tried specific feedback strategies with students, and reported an improvement in students' attitudes and academic performance. It is important to note that both of these examples, as was true with others, represented an intersection between the CLC initiative and other initiatives in the schools—the former, a project using a lesson-study approach to embedding formative assessment to improve student learning; the latter, built on earlier local work in action research.

There was a positive trend in survey respondents' views of their school cultures in the second year of implementation compared to the first year's data.[3] However, organizational impact varied across sites; at this point, there was far less evidence of this than of individual impacts. There seemed to be a pervasive assumption among participants that the collaborative values and processes of CLCs would spread virus-like in the schools and districts in which they were situated, or would have a "trickle-down" effect. (See the next section for discussion.) There seemed to be four categories of organizational impact: (1) CLCs as oases of collaborative culture; (2) nurturing natural possibilities for using protocols; (3) strategic development of collaborative cultures; and (4) mandating participation.

As previously noted, successful CLCs have developed a collaborative culture within their groups. But even in schools with a number of CLCs, the groups sometimes remained oases for their members without influencing the culture and practices of the larger organization. As one coach commented, "In our CLC we have tremendous support, but once you walk out that door, you don't have that." A new CLC in a new alternative program created a life raft for teachers and support staff who were working with extremely challenging young people. In addition to their weekly CLC meetings, they had been meeting in the morning and at the end of the school day to plan and debrief, which they found essential to their own and students' success. The program was eliminated the next school year.

"Nurturing the natural possibilities," CLC coaches and members used CLC strategies in classrooms, workshops, and meetings, thus capitalizing on naturally occurring ad hoc opportunities to use collaborative protocols for professional dialogue. Enthusiastic use of protocols also occurred in church groups, as well as at parent and community meetings.

Taking this nurturance of possibilities to the next level, there were some examples of strategically embedding CLC processes in efforts to develop more collaborative cultures in schools and districts. In schools where principals provided leadership by modeling and encouraging professional dialogue, there was a sense among staff of a shift in the culture and deeper, more productive discussion about supporting students' and adults' learning, and that "It's okay to not know the answer and to ask for help." A principal noted that she has changed the focus of meetings as one element of her strategy to change school culture:

> I use best practices of CLCs and of professional learning communities in staff meetings. I even changed the name to change the thinking about what we do when we come together. But I don't label it as Lucent or CLC or anything. The educators would see that as something new they have to do. . . . I am planting the seed of bringing stuff out of the classroom into public view. That is a mental shift for teachers.

In administrative CLCs, members found a safe space to share dilemmas and resources. As one district administrator noted:

> Administrative people are experiencing the process, and therefore if they decide to, it becomes possible to spread it to their buildings . . . because these folks have already been part of it.

A subject-area supervisor changed the way she worked with teachers to improve curriculum and instruction with an eye to bolstering student achievement by embedding structured conversations with a particular focus over time and expected that this would become the norm for the way professional work is done in this content area. Others responsible for professional development of experienced and novice teachers also have, over time, taken a strategic approach in embedding collaborative processes in their work with educators. The key difference between this more strategic approach and the "natural possibilities" approach is that it took a deliberate, long-term view toward creating a collaborative culture focused on improving learning for adults and children, rather than being ad hoc. Both are important, but ad hoc activity alone is unlikely to have significant organizational impact.

One district, in its effort to spread the CLC work district-wide, required school facilitators to attend a coaching group and to use protocols with educators in the schools with which they work. In a couple of instances, principals mandated the use of protocols school-wide. In one middle school, all staff were members of one of three CLCs—all coached by an administrator. Can compliance result in collaboration? This remains to be seen. As one person commented, requiring people to participate in the beginning may lead to them seeing the value and wanting to work this way.

In addition to impacts on individuals and the schools where they worked, three elements of the New Jersey CLC Initiative also targeted development of within- and cross-district capacity: a cross-district leadership CLC; cross-district "tunings" of annual plans; and the development of a cadre of "lead facilitators."

The cross-district CLC, or "3DCLC," brought district leaders together three or four times a year for collaborative dialogue about their work to support the integration of the CLCs in their schools and districts—not as a "project" but as a way of working. Composed of assistant superintendents, curriculum directors, and project coordinators, the group addressed issues highlighted previously, shared ideas and strategies, and explored the implications of developing more collaborative cultures in organizations that have long been largely hierarchical. Members of the 3DCLC found these gatherings valuable and perhaps, as they discussed in one meeting, the only venue in which Abbott and non-Abbott districts were talking about substantive issues of change. Unfortunately, only one district had stable membership in this group from year to year, while the other two districts sent new representatives each year.

The project director convened annual "tuning meetings" for teams from each district. The intent of these meetings was to present the teams' plans for the next year for feedback from the other districts prior to submitting them to the foundation. As with the 3DCLC, these meetings provided fertile ground for exchanging ideas and opening up new ways of thinking about professional collaboration that paralleled the work of educators in CLCs. Districts borrowed ideas and strategies from one another and even collaborated on a federal grant.

In the second year, each district identified two experienced CLC coaches to "apprentice" to the external facilitator, and added two more in the third year. The goal of developing this cadre of "lead facilitators" was to strengthen capacity at the district and cross-district level to continue support for the CLCs beyond the grant period. The "lead facilitators" took increasing roles in leadership planning and in leading cross-district coaches' seminars. In one district, the lead facilitators' professional roles allowed them to incorporate this responsibility fairly seamlessly; in the other two districts, questions remain about how the districts will capitalize on their expertise in future years.

We heard many testimonials about the impact on CLC coaches' and members' personal and interpersonal skills, knowledge, and dispositions, as well as some about efforts to infuse various groups, schools, and districts with CLC processes and to create more collaborative cultures. We heard far less about the impact on student learning than on adult dispositions and dialogues. One district leader noted that there is "not a direct line between collaboration and student achievement, but how we work together and examine practice and results . . . eventually will translate into improved student achievement." We would suggest that a more deliberate connection must be made.

MULTIPLE AND MISSING THEORIES OF ACTION

Voluntary or mandatory participation? During the day or after school? Naturally occurring or newly formed, cross-role groups? Facilitate adult talk or examine student work? Go slow, or dive in?

The previous two sections presented a wide array of arrangements and impacts as well as a variety of contextual circumstances. An appropriate and a key question to ask at the end of the initiative is: Do these variations represent innovative strategies for ultimately improving student learning, or are they "practical" accommodations to more pressing priorities? That is, are decision makers (whether district officials, building administrators, or CLC facilitators) creatively exploring a myriad of possibilities for forming and operating CLCs effectively, or are they forcing CLCs to function within local constraints, regardless of whether those ways of functioning actually benefit the group, their workplaces, and/or students? If the answer to the former half of the two questions is affirmative, then one might be justified in thinking that all of the differences are simply normal and expected outgrowths of developing CLCs. If the latter halves of the questions depict the situation, then the conclusion should probably be that after several years, CLCs remain relatively minor blips on the districts' radar screens.

All of this begs an even larger question: *Where do all of these actions and arrangements fit in the scheme to improve student achievement?* For example, what is the logical path from having voluntary CLCs meet after school six times a year to altering teachers' instructional practices? Or, what is the connection between having subject-area coordinators meet regularly—using protocols—and raising student achievement? In other words, do participants share a theory of change that lodges their decisions and actions in well-defined places along a chain of events that people are confident will lead to better instructional experiences for students?

The interview data say "No." Everyone, of course, acknowledged that the only reason to engage in any serious, concerted enterprise in their districts was to benefit students, but it is unclear, at best, whether a sizable number of participants agreed on how CLCs should be structured and operated to attain that goal. For example, in one district, several people spoke of CLCs as becoming "embedded processes" that occurred within naturally occurring groups, such as middle school teams or high school SLCs, thereby enhancing already occurring conversations. Thus the end goal was improved dialogue, and not just creating CLCs. However, no such "natural" groups meet in the elementary schools, and participation there dropped with the advent of the after-school formula—and none of the people interviewed at that level could articulate a viable alternative unless "the district changes its mind." So, is embedding the process a vehicle for change that works at one level but not another? And which vehicle will work at the elementary level, since the consensus was that the after-school model does not work very well?

Similar questions could be posed with respect to the already noted situations in the other two districts. For example, in one district, a couple of principals modeled protocols in faculty meetings and expected those processes to be used in other meetings as a result. Was this strategy an individually devised method of improving educators' conversations, or was it the manifestation of some larger design that proposed that several principals "pilot" a means for involving entire schools in CLC-like activities? Another district, on the other hand, had schools where some staff members were in a CLC and some not. Again, was this arrangement an outgrowth of an espoused change strategy that stated that a single CLC could ultimately influence school-wide behavior? Or, did all of this reflect a situation similar to what one participant experienced in the first year of the initiative: "We were just going along; no one knew what this was."

The above questions are not intended to be rhetorical. However, at best, there are multiple theories of change—implicit and explicit—circulating within and across the districts and between and among individuals. At worst, of course, no "big picture" of causality and consequences exists. And, as much as people seem to accept readily the value of reflecting on one's actions, little formal examination of the various arrangements and their impacts has taken place—according to the interviews at least. In fact, most participants—there are exceptions, particularly in some buildings—say that they "have no idea" about what the future holds for CLCs in their districts—a telling commentary on whether any communal notion of how everything fits together exists.

Although not a theory of change, one assumption about how CLCs and students are connected does seem to underlie much of what people said, and that is: "If educators talk more productively about what students do and think in the classroom, then teachers' reflections about those conversations will lead to altering instruction in ways that improve student learning." For example, one person said that the connection to learning was through "teachers talking about their teaching; it affects learning by teachers tweaking what they already do." For this talk to accomplish that end, it needs to have "a particular focus" and consist of "structured conversations, solution-oriented, not just free conversation." Another person elaborated further:

> Teachers get very excited about being able to cluster around similar concerns and really drive the conversation. Empowerment is almost magical, so invigorating, and they get very excited about these conversations. *However*, we can't ignore the crux of the conversation, and that is what we are seeing in the classroom when we look at the work that students are doing. We have to balance all that excitement and energy and teacher-driven work with "Why? What's it all about? Anchor it with what is actually coming from the hands, the mouths, the minds of the kids."

Similar statements arise all the time—in interviews, in coaches' CLCs, in the seminars, and so on. People proposed that talk leads to change. What is missing in nearly all of these statements, however, is a clear idea of *how* that might happen. For instance, theories of organizational and personal change often contain stages—for example, examination, reflection, decision, and then action. These stages are invariably portrayed as cyclical rather than linear. That is, change occurs through "repeated" run-throughs of this process. The "talk leads to change" assumption does not contain even implicitly ideas about what happens after the person reflects, such as how the person reaches a decision about what to change, what data the person must collect to see if the change worked, when and where the person can represent what happened to the CLC, and how a CLC can accommodate one person's trip through the reflective cycle—much less all of the members.

Thus people have been fuzzy about how to get "from here to there," on two levels: the eventual role (and fate) of CLCs at the organizational level and collectively improving practice at the school level.

Actually, people tend to espouse "visions" more than "plans of action." These visions are grand and hopeful:

> This is about adults being able to look at themselves as works in progress. What happens is openness to different perspectives. If we can do that with colleagues, kids have to benefit from that.
>
> It's a wonderful thing, time to reflect. Schools would be very different places.
>
> You're planting seeds through using [processes] in faculty meetings, workshops, building in time for reflections; and people are amazed at how that makes the experience so much richer.
>
> We've learned the importance of sharing good practices, opening our doors, letting people know we're challenged and have opportunities to talk about it. The school is becoming a community where we learn from one another, tearing down the walls that have been up for so long.

But the best they can come up with as a strategy for achieving these desirable states is: "You have to experience it. Once you do it, it's addictive. You can't imagine doing it any other way." Or, as another person claimed, "It's hard work, but it leads to systemic change, growth and advancement. It's so powerful you have to experience it yourself."

In summary, theories of change/action operating in the districts are not widely shared or even concretely stated. It is beyond question that people see power in the CLCs, but their visions contain more unrestrained hope than strategic thought. This does not bode well for either embedding CLCs or expanding CLCs with the intention of increasing student achievement, especially in situations where change has been so elusive in the past. The final question to ask, then, is: So how will this time be different?

CONCLUSION

Numerous educational change initiatives wind up in reform cemeteries, full of tombstones with epitaphs capturing their demise, mostly saying "the money ran out" or "something else came up." But positive outcomes do exist, and not all reforms eventually fall prey to the ravages of stern challenges. While it may be too early to offer a prognosis for the districts in the Alcatel-Lucent Foundation Initiative, it is clear that they will succeed to the extent that participants figure out how to tie their adult conversations more directly to student learning.

Several CLCs have made this step, and such developments might serve as a useful starting place for devising effective theories of action. For example, a group of high school science teachers—focusing on embedding formative assessment in order to enhance student understanding and achievement—has explored the literature and formative assessment strategies, tried them out in the classroom, and brought back to their group student work and reports on how their strategies worked. They discuss these, then tune their strategies and go back to their classrooms again, creating a continuous loop between the work of the CLC and improvement of professional practice and students' learning.

Members of a middle school CLC noticed that they were complaining about students' poor attitudes and then recognized that their own attitudes toward their classes were not entirely positive. As a result, they decided to explore the role of attitude in learning. After reading and discussing some relevant articles, they tried out some strategies, such as giving students positive and specific feedback. Everyone reported back and brought student work to the CLC and saw very positive changes. They broke down the curriculum—from unit design to lesson plan to products—to identify where and how they could best support students' success, and they continued to try out, over time, various strategies with the students. They reported that in addition to more positive attitudes, students' academic performance improved.

Instituting a new literacy curriculum this year, a fourth-grade team studied the curriculum materials, tried and tuned instructional strategies, and examined student work and assessment results. The coach reported that students' writing had improved, that the students had gained confidence, and that the students' performance scores rose significantly on a standardized reading assessment.

In each of these examples, key elements supported the CLCs' success. We would argue that there are at least several factors at work:

- having an image of the connections between adults collaborating and students learning
- establishing a clear purpose/shared focus that is compelling to the group members
- drawing on exemplary outside resources relevant to their focus
- using a cycle of planning, acting, and reviewing the results tied directly to their focus and work with students or adults

- having adequate time to do the work
- providing support from building and district administration that this work is of primary importance

It is clear from the efforts of the districts that there is a strong will on the part of nearly every participant to have this work improve student learning. There is unquestioned enthusiasm and commitment by those who have been touched directly by the work of CLCs. But as the initiative finishes the final year of the Alcatel-Lucent Foundation support, there are still critical challenges that must be confronted. An essential next step is to make the connection between student learning and adults working together in new and more productive ways. To be sure, nearly everyone espouses and believes the mantra that "the ultimate goal is student achievement." In order for this vision to be realized, however, participants will have to produce a road map that makes the connections from adults working together more productively to students' higher achievement. Several CLCs offer glimmers of hope that this task is both doable and necessary. It remains the responsibility of all participants to turn these initial steps into shimmering success throughout their districts.

NOTES

1. The external documentation team collected data through observation of the summer institute and winter retreat of all district teams; observation of at least two LDT sessions in each district; informal and formal interviews with LDT members, other key district personnel and LDT coaches; and review of LDT internal documentation. Documentation team members also listened in on monthly facilitators' conference calls and communicated regularly with the project director. Coordination with internal documenters took place throughout the year via e-mail, phone, and face-to-face meetings.

2. The design originally involved a fourth suburban district; after one year of implementation, however, this district had a change of leadership, along with which came a new set of instructional and administrative priorities.

3. At the end of each year of implementation, the participants in all of the CLCs are asked to complete a survey. The questions are adapted from a survey developed by Jane H. Huffman and Kristine K. Hipp, *Reculturing Schools as Professional Learning Communities* (Lanham, MD: Scarecrow Education, 2003).

৫ 6 ৩৯

DEEPENING THE WORK

Promise and Perils of Collaborative Inquiry

DIANE R. WOOD

There is a widening consensus that the quality of students' educational experiences has everything to do with the quality of their teachers. While opinions differ about how to ensure "quality," most of those writing about improving schools agree that top-quality teachers know how to craft engaging, effective learning experiences for students despite shifting demographic, social, and economic conditions. Because constant change is a condition of teachers' lives, the most effective teachers must keep their knowledge current and useful. For the best teachers, ongoing professional learning simply must become an essential aspect of their work.

Recognizing this, the literature of school change increasingly contains recommendations that teacher learning be organized around professional learning communities (Allen, Blythe and Thompson-Grove 2004; Calderwood 2000; DuFour and Eaker 1998; Lieberman and Wood 2002; McLaughlin and Talbert 2001; Westheimer 1998; Weinbaum, Allen, and Blythe 2004). At the heart of such recommendations is a compelling notion of teacher professionalism that casts teachers as not only *users* of pedagogical knowledge but also as *creators* of it, as not only effective practitioners but also as career-long learners, as not only coaches and guides for students but also as constructive collaborators with colleagues. How does participation in a learning community give teachers opportunities to enact this vision of the teacher's role? Under what conditions does the experience advance this vision of teacher professionalism? Do teachers embrace or reject these roles? What are the promises and the perils when they try?

119

In order to delve into these questions, this chapter begins by tracing the work of two teachers who facilitated learning communities. Realizing the potential of collective inquiry as a process for structuring and deepening the efforts of teachers in their respective learning communities to improve their practices and improve student learning, they worked to instantiate it as a core process. Their story, then, is about a struggle to replace the quest for certainty with a "stance of inquiry" (Cochran-Smith and Lytle 2001), about the obstacles and barriers they encountered, and about how they and their colleagues came to embrace new professional roles and responsibilities for student learning. In the process, many participants developed a new vision of teacher professionalism.

In an effort to harvest as much understanding as possible from their story, the chapter parses the concept "professional learning community" through the lens of teacher professionalism and the role collective inquiry might play in enhancing it. As DuFour and Eaker (1998) have written, each word in that phrase—*professional, learning,* and *community*—defines an essential dimension of these groups. This chapter explores these three dimensions and concludes with an analysis of the obstacles that professional learning communities can encounter along the way.

REDEFINING PROFESSIONAL RESPONSIBILITY

After having been facilitators of LLCs in their school for two years, Joanne, a literacy specialist, and Karen, a classroom teacher, spoke enthusiastically about the positive impact of the LLCs. Teachers, they claimed, were growing more positive about meeting in collegial groups, and they were beginning to recognize why sharing challenges in their teaching might be helpful. Most of the resistance to the LLCs had, according to Karen, "faded away." This success was heartening for Karen and Joanne, whose school served a diverse student population with many English-language learners. It was also known for low test scores, and three fourths of its students lived in poverty. In fact, the district's former superintendent had selected Lincoln Elementary School to participate in the Peer Collaboration Initiative precisely *because* of these unpromising conditions. She had also recognized that Yvette, Lincoln's principal, was a strong, visionary leader. For Yvette and teacher leaders like Joanne and Karen, the LLCs became the "great hope" to rally the adults in the school around improving student learning.

Despite an auspicious beginning working with their learning communities, by the end of the second year both Karen and Joanne described a nagging suspicion that something was missing. Joanne put it this way:

> We're doing great with [community building], but what I'm thinking is: Is that *all* we're doing? I'm afraid that's the way it's playing out in some of the groups in our school. I'm wondering for myself [as a facilitator]: Have I gotten it balanced? Am I doing too much community building? But I do know it's paid off. Our group is really comfortable with each other; last year they hated working together. And they're starting to ask good questions. Still, we need to go deeper.

Karen expressed a similar ambivalence, "Joanne said it beautifully. We're building community, but we're just beginning to discover the true meaning of the LLCs."

For both Joanne and Karen, the "true meaning" of the LLCs was clear: the improvement of teaching for the sake of student learning. But in their district there were different accountability systems pressing on teachers to ensure this same result. On the one hand, the state had their district (and all districts) under close scrutiny to raise students' test scores under the No Child Left Behind legislation. Meeting those demands, according to the state and to the district curriculum developer, required fidelity to "research-based best practices," according to the district curriculum developer. On the other hand, the LLC initiative asked teachers to openly discuss their thinking and practices, critique and improve them, and then share student work as evidence that students were learning. Collaboration in that spirit, they thought, must involve more than friendly—even trusting—collegial relationships. Teachers could not simply come together for community building; they would have to come together to ask hard questions about what they were doing and why (Dewey 2007; Giroux 1988; Hargreaves 1991; Grumet 1988; Schon 1983).

The question became: Would it be possible for teachers to serve both masters? Could they faithfully comply with outside expertise and also develop the habits of mind and dialogue necessary for ongoing inquiry? Should teachers be enactors of others' expertise, or critical, questioning collaborators? Which version of teacher professionalism should prevail? Having been introduced to the idea of collective inquiry during an LLC facilitators' meeting in Maine, Joanne and Karen were optimistic that they could take the latter approach. They left that meeting eager to convince their colleagues to try to deepen their work through collective inquiry.

MOVING FROM COMMUNITY BUILDING
TO COLLABORATIVE INQUIRY

Karen and Joanne recognized that building trust among LLC group members was essential if teachers were to feel free to bring challenges and problems to the group for open discussion. They were right, of course, because for any innovation involving teacher collaboration to take hold, the "regularities" of teacher individualism and isolation (Lieberman and Miller 1999; Lortie 1975; Sarason 1991, 1996) must be disrupted and transformed. After two years as coaches, however, both Joanne and Karen conceded that their concern for "safety" had resulted in using too many relationship-building activities for too long. Joanne put it this way: "That idea of community building. We're doing that, but what I'm thinking is: Is that all we're doing?" In their emphasis on trust and safety, they had not settled deeply enough into the hard work of actually linking teaching practices to improving student learning.

It was not that Joanne and Karen had not pushed for this larger agenda. Indeed, they had introduced a variety of "protocols" provided by the National School Reform Faculty (NSRF) to facilitate discussions around individuals' dilemmas of practice and for analyzing student work and determining pedagogical "next steps." They had used "tuning protocols" to critically assess lesson plans, assessment strategies, and various assignments. In their determination to take advantage of available resources, they came to realize that they had chosen breadth of exposure to protocols over the depth of using a few of them well (Wood 2007).

There were also the attendant problems involved with "scaling up" a reform effort. At first the LLCs were voluntary, though the target schools had always planned to eventually promote 100 percent participation. The next year, as more staff members received training as coaches, Yvette, Lincoln's principal, told teachers they could either join an LLC or work with other teachers to design another collaborative option. By the third year, the LLC work did indeed become mandatory. And Yvette and her leadership team decided that the LLCs should be reconfigured to accommodate 100 percent participation. Rather than use "vertical groups" that brought together teachers from all grade levels and roles (e.g., specialists, instructional facilitators), LLC work would be conducted in the twice-monthly grade-level meetings. This configuration of the groups ensured common, relevant, and immediate concerns for all participants; it also made the groups much smaller—approximately five to eight people instead of twelve to fifteen, as in previous years.

Perhaps predictably, mandatory participation resulted in passive (and sometimes outright) resistance in the school's LLCs. In Joanne's and Karen's LLCs, however, participants enthusiastically engaged in stimulating conversations about the special challenges of working with the students in their school. They talked intently about books they read together, and they began swapping instructional strategies. According to both Karen and Joanne, during this third year the habits and benefits of collaboration were beginning to permeate the culture of their groups. This was especially evident, they said, in the kinds of questions participants were raising about their teaching.

Because of the December meeting in Maine, Joanne and Karen began the second semester of the school year determined to engage their LLCs in collective inquiry. Unexpected circumstances, however, dampened their initial enthusiasm. Meetings were interrupted by school closings due to weather or because the district usurped the time for other pressing business. Karen and Joanne could not even find the time to introduce the notion of inquiry to the group until early March; once they finally had their opportunity, however, their enthusiasm returned. Fortunately, Joanne and Karen had good command of the principles and processes behind a strategy—taught during the December meeting—known as the "cycle of inquiry." Adapting it for their specific purposes, they used a form called a "Team Learning Log," which required LLCs to name an instructional problem based on empirical data, to generate solutions likely to make an empirical difference, and to articulate an action plan, including an assessment of the process.

Karen, herself a fifth-grade teacher, worked with the other fifth-grade teachers in the school. As literacy coach, Joanne facilitated an LLC with the kindergarten team. Both LLCs, after some deliberation, eventually established a common focus for their inquiry. They went through several processes of articulating problems, generating action plans, implementing the plans, documenting what happened, and then bringing their data to subsequent meetings. In interviews, participants deemed the meetings "productive," "helpful," "worthwhile," and even "necessary." During an interview with Karen and Joanne, Karen said:

> I feel like even though our group's been restructured this year and we've just worked together on inquiry really one year, we're there. Even though it's not called "the cycle of inquiry," we are seeing a need, asking what we can do about it, making an action plan, following through with that action plan in our

instruction, and then assessing what we've done and thinking about that need and what we need to do next. We're trying to keep our questions and our needs small enough that we can see a result. Before we had questions that were so huge—or so many questions—that we couldn't see *anything*. But now we've got this problem-solving approach. We see a need that sparks an action plan, and the action plan gives us some data that shows us another need and that sparks another action plan. . . . I guess that's really the cycle of inquiry.

Nevertheless, there were arresting differences among the various LLCs at Lincoln, including differences between the two groups facilitated by Joanne and Karen. One key difference was that Karen's group could articulate *why LLC work was worthwhile*, while Joanne's group could not. For instance, during a focus group interview, Karen's fifth-grade team, which had five participants, eagerly discussed the professional purpose and value of the LLCs. They talked about how they were able to make better decisions, respond more effectively to students' individual needs, create more engaging lessons, and make their expectations and explanations clearer and more accessible. Because they made the rationale behind their choices explicit in their LLCs, they found themselves doing the same for their students. One teacher said, "I find I am making my own thinking more transparent to the kids. They see the thinking behind the lesson." All agreed that the collection of data disciplined their thinking and judgment, forcing them to weigh their opinions in light of empirical evidence. As one teacher put it simply, "We're all learning; we're all feeling more professional."

In a separate focus group that same week, however, when asked about the purpose for their LLC, the kindergarten teachers eagerly listed specific strategies they had used to try to improve kindergartners' literacy. Even when pressed, they couldn't seem to define an overall purpose; follow-up questions simply generated more lists of strategies. Over time, as the research team watched different LLCs operate, we realized that the difference between these two groups exemplifies two different ways in which LLC work can be conceptualized. In Karen's group, the fifth-grade teachers had developed and internalized a set of values associated with their experiences in their LLCs, and they had developed the following habits of mind and practice that they were also able to articulate as "professional": a focus on learning and learners, continuous questioning about what would engage learners and improve their learning, informed, data-driven decision making, and the importance of making the thinking behind their own professional choices transparent to both colleagues and students

Moreover, a year later, the fifth graders' scores on the state's standardized test met state requirements for the first time in four years.

Unlike the fifth-grade team, the kindergarten team seemed to view the LLCs more as a repository and/or generator of helpful strategies. While the fifth-grade team was developing a conception of the professional teacher as thinker, inquirer, and builder of knowledge, the kindergarten team focused more on implementation. To understand the impact of this difference in Karen's and Joanne's teams, it is helpful to turn, once again, to the phrase "professional learning community" in some detail.

PROFESSIONAL LEARNING COMMUNITIES THROUGH THE LENS OF COLLECTIVE INQUIRY

Contemporary progressive educators (Cochran-Smith and Lytle 1999, 2001; Goodlad 1984; Greene 1988; Grumet 1988; McDonald et al. 2003; McLaughlin and Talbert 2001) have argued convincingly, as did Dewey (1916), that the professional collaboration of teachers ought to lead to the collective investigation of problems embedded in classroom practice. Today this call for collaboration is often expressed in terms of "professional learning communities." Given the widespread use of this phrase, however, its meaning needs careful examination, particularly as it is related to LLCs. Parsing the phrase "professional learning community," the following three questions seem especially crucial:

1. What kind of *professional* teacher is most likely to help LLCs meet their primary goal of improving student learning?
2. What kind of professional learning must take place in an LLC?
3. How should we define community within an LLC?

What kind of professional *teacher is most likely to help LLCs meet their primary goal of improving student learning?*

Despite the fact that *professional* learning communities are often recommended for teachers, controversy persists over whether teaching is actually a profession. Lortie (1975) argued that teaching as a profession has always been "special but shadowed"—a poorly paid but badly needed occupation that, by turns, can be either revered or scorned. More recently, Grant and Murray (1999) have claimed that a profession gains recognition and respect due to the extent and value of the expertise held by its members. Efforts such as that of the National Board for Professional Teaching Standards aim to raise the status of teaching precisely by claiming that teachers hold expertise and then mobilizing teachers in an effort to make that expertise public.

Typically, professions have the following five characteristics, besides serving a valuable function for society: (1) special knowledge, (2) authority, (3) self-regulation, (4) a code of ethics, and (5) public trust. Schon (1983) argues that "reflective practitioners" are constantly building knowledge as they go about their work, and he agrees with Elbaz (1983) that this knowledge is largely tacit. Thus the knowledge of teachers often lies unrecognized, unexpressed, unpublicized—and, ultimately, unappreciated. Teachers who work in bureaucratic schools and districts may wield authority inside the classroom but seldom outside. Clearly, the work of teachers is not self-regulating. Most decisions about licensure, hiring, induction, retention, and tenure are made from outside the teaching ranks. There is no code of ethics that governs the work of teachers, as there is for, say, lawyers and doctors. The constant media harangue against public schooling reflects little public trust in teachers. In short, the status of teaching as a profession is ambiguous, just as Lortie said more than thirty years ago.

Recognizing this, Gutmann (1999) argues that public schools cannot serve a democracy without investing more authority in teachers. She, like others (Grumet 1988; Hargreaves 1994; Hofmann 1981), posits that the work of teaching has taken shape as "women's work" since the nineteenth century, when the country mobilized a universal public education effort to socialize newly arrived immigrants and the poor. Lured into the field because of their so-called "natural" ability to nurture children, the women who became teachers entered bureaucratic, hierarchical institutions where they had little authority or decision-making power. Calling for dramatic change, Gutmann (1999) argues for a "democratic professionalism" that avoids the "insolence" that comes from too much authority (i.e., too little dialogue with the general public because of arrogance about professional expertise) or the "ossification" of having too little authority (i.e., becoming rigid and resistant to change because of too much outside control and intervention). The teaching profession, Gutmann suggests, falls in the latter category. She claims that teachers need to have authority to "shed critical light on a democratically created culture" (76), but that this authority needs to be tempered by critical dialogue with peers, students, parents, and the general public.

The LLCs represent one step toward engaging teachers in exactly this sort of dialogue; as a result, they have the potential to actually contribute to the professionalization of teaching. In fact, those who argue for learning communities claim that, at their best, they provide a venue for releasing and constructing knowledge with the potential to improve schools (Cochran-Smith and Lytle 1999; McDonald et al. 2003). Instead of seeing the responsibility for "knowing what to do" as lying with administrators, consultants, or professors, teachers can begin to shoulder the responsibility to search collectively for their own answers, using whatever resources they deem helpful. This amounts to a major shift in notions of accountability. Instead of mere compliance with demands coming from outside the profession, teachers are more likely to *internalize* a sense of collective responsibility for their students' learning, perhaps a far more effective form of accountability in that it becomes less coercive and dependent on exterior control and more a matter of an urgent and informed sense of moral responsibility.

Joanne and Karen understood this potential. Both wanted to see teachers making decisions based on both lived experience *and* empirical evidence, which they referred to simply as "data." In interviews, they defined data broadly as test scores, student work samples, and observations of students. Karen, who was already in the habit of poring over such data to make adjustments in her teaching, began to share data samples in her LLC. In doing so, she pioneered the way for the others to do the same. Karen described the process in this way: "I've always had this sense that I have a huge responsibility to do my best and to do my best for the kids. . . . Now, with LLCs, it's maybe admitting that I'm not doing my best, and can you [professional colleagues] help me to do my best?"

Part of the struggle for Joanne and Karen was realizing that *their* notion of what it means to be a professional teacher was not initially shared by most of the key players in their school, district, and larger community (teachers, administrators, state officials, and the general public). In fact, Joanne's and Karen's emerging sense of professionalism runs counter to typical school cultures, according to many sociologies of teaching (Cohn and Kottkamp 1993; Goodlad 1984; Lortie 1975; Sarason 1996; Waller 1967 [1932]). Schools tend to socialize teachers to see professionalism as following rules and procedures, dressing appropriately, and managing students without complaint. In an interview, Joanne reflected on how she was taught as a young teacher not to ask too many questions or to air her teaching concerns:

I think back to my last year in the classroom. I was always wondering what can I do better? What am I not doing that I could be doing? My principal's observations always came back positive. But I really wanted to know. My first-grade kids—most of them ELL [English Language Learners] kids—had the lowest scores. I asked one of the literacy teachers when she came into the room, "What can I do with my teaching of writing to make it better?" And she didn't answer. . . . And you know I was so embarrassed I didn't ask the question again of someone else. (Interview, February 2004)

Since then, Joanne's LLC experiences have given her an alternative vision for schools where teachers' questions are discussed rather than stifled. She says now: "[LLCs] have really helped me get back to asking the questions out loud, and when they [LLCs] work, they help everyone else also to be okay with asking questions or being asked questions."

After the meeting in Maine, Joanne and Karen struggled to get their groups to "own" collective processes of critical dialogue and inquiry as being central to their work. This would require, according to Karen, "new professional dispositions," such as the capacity for self-critique. As an example, she told a story about a "know-it-all" novice teacher with whom she had recently socialized outside of school. This brand-new teacher told Karen that she, in the process of a formal review, rated herself *excellent* in all phases of her teaching. Incredulous, Karen mused, "How can *any* teacher think they're doing great in everything—much less one so inexperienced?" She went on to say that some teachers seemed more interested in *defending* their practices and hiding their mistakes than openly admitting their struggles. Perhaps this is especially true, she surmised, when teachers know they work under critical surveillance because of state and federal accountability policies.

For Karen, professional teaching practice is not just a matter of simple competence. It means broadening a narrow focus on *what* to do (strategies) to include *why* I am doing what I'm doing and *how* might I do it better. As she put it:

Before the LLCs, my way of collaborating was doing all the *whats* and sharing all the *whats*. And now it's about asking the *whys*. I still think the *whats* are important, and sometimes I need to do the *whats* in order to understand the *whys*. I learn from modeling and watching people. But now I'm growing, and I'm thinking more about *why* should I do this or that, and could I do it some other way? Try something else? Is this *really* doing what I want it to do? Is this really, *really* the way I want to help kids?

This tension—whether or not teachers should be invested with the *whys* of practice as well as the *whats*—has everything to do with professionalism. Teachers willing to base decisions about their practice on solid reasoning, accumulating expertise, collaborative dialogue, and outside research develop the authority and autonomy to act in students' best interests.

Because Karen wanted to nurture a growing sense of professional autonomy and authority in her colleagues, she worried that Yvette's decision to reconfigure the LLCs might undermine her efforts. Instead of being an opportunity that teachers could choose, the LLCs became one more thing with which to comply. According to Karen:

> Some of the original spirit and original purpose has been lost because of the crisis situation [raising test scores as the state demanded]. We would have loved to have had our own [LLC]. We would have known the purpose behind it, but the rest of the school is just so under the gun that there's no time for this. We have immediate needs. For some grade-level groups, it's working out okay. But there are some who just don't see the purpose, and they think it's just one more thing they have to do. (Interview, January 2004)

Despite having reservations about reconfiguring the groups and making them mandatory, Joanne and Karen had no trouble seeing how what they learned in their LLCs could be transferred to grade-level meetings. Joanne commented, "I see that what we learned isn't just LLC protocols. This is about expanding these ideas into all of what I do." By facilitating the LLCs for a couple of years, Joanne and Karen had begun to internalize a new set of values, attitudes, and dispositions. They saw that the protocols were simply tools to structure conversations; the reason for having those conversations in the first place was what really mattered.

As explained earlier, there was a key difference in their relationship to their groups, however. Joanne, as a literacy coach, had a supervisory relationship with her group, while Karen, as another fifth-grade teacher, was seen as a peer by the fifth-grade team. While both grade-level LLCs eventually undertook the cycle of inquiry, the kindergarten team looked to Joanne to guide them. The fifth-grade team undertook the process as equals and began to rotate facilitation, eventually recognizing how undertaking a stance of inquiry demanded a different professional mind-set. Karen's group was the only LLC facilitated by a classroom teacher (the others were facilitated by instructional coaches, specialists, or administrators), and it seemed, in fact, to exercise the most autonomy.

As they gained a new sense of what it meant to be a professional teacher, the participants in Karen's LLC had mixed reactions to the impact of accountability determined by test scores. On the one hand, they confessed that the outside pressure of the tests (all fifth graders are tested in their state) "keeps us very focused," as one teacher said. Others indicated, however, that it was actually the LLC work that helped them cope with the pressure and ensured that they maintained a focus on high-quality instruction, not just test preparation. The fifth-grade team was mixed as to whether the motivation to raise test scores made their group effective or whether the real value of LLC participation was finding ways to buffer students from the negative impact of high-stakes testing. One participant praised the "sense of confidence and comfort" the group had established, which enabled them to discuss hard issues and decide how to proceed. She said, "With all this pressure, I can focus on what's good for kids."

This capacity to keep "thinking about the kids," along with "talking about the whys," they said, helped them mount particularly persuasive arguments when they approached the administration to garner support for their ideas. Both the principal and the vice principal were impressed, they said, with their capacity to articulate a rationale when they wanted to take a particular approach—one based on a commitment to student learning:

> Now we discuss what we want to do and we do it openly and get everything out on the table, and so when we do go out to an administrator, we have already discussed it, we've already talked it through, we've thought about all the ifs, ands, or buts. And we are presenting it as a front . . . as all of us saying this— not just one person, this is all of us. . . . I think other teams who don't have this sense of comfort . . . can't proceed as well as we have. Being "comfortable" with each other to say the harder stuff means having confidence. (Karen's Focus Group, February 2004)

This newly gained confidence recalls Gutmann's recommendation for teachers to develop a greater sense of authority, efficacy, and autonomy while also retaining a sense of accountability to those the profession is supposed to serve. Yvette, the principal, said that the fifth-grade LLC was "among the best," fostering good judgment and solid professional work; she confirmed what both Karen and Joanne said about their LLCs making a difference in teachers' practices.

In separate interviews, Yvette and Karen described *how* the LLCs had made that difference and referred to the same story in the process. Apparently, Yvette went into Karen's classroom for a routine observation, and, in Karen's words:

> I did a reading activity and I didn't give her [Yvette] what she wanted to see, and she gave me good critical feedback on that. And so I worked for awhile and then I said, "Come and watch me again." . . . Then I said, "Come and watch me a third time." And I wanted the critical feedback, and it was okay if I made mistakes. I wanted to get better. I don't think I would have done that if I didn't have the language and tools that I learned through the LLCs. And there were times I'd disagree with Yvette and then we'd talk it out.

Telling a similar version of this story, Yvette said, "I know Karen 'gets it'" (Interview, February 2004). Yvette went on to explain that Karen understood she would have to continually question her teaching practices in order to meet students' evolving needs, and Karen was not ashamed to invite others' advice, criticism, and suggestions.

Karen had learned to access and use for her own purposes, rather than simply submit to, Yvette's expertise and supervisory role; she saw Yvette's insights and authority as good for her own professional development and good for the children in her class. Rather than simply complying with Yvette's expectations, she began to set some of her own terms and ask for Yvette's critique. As Yvette experienced the fifth-grade teachers taking more ownership of their own practices, she ceded increasing space for Karen and her group to exercise autonomy and authority. As Yvette explained in an interview, this was exactly the level of professionalism she wanted to see in teachers.

Joanne, who wanted to see that level of professionalism in the kindergarten teachers who participated in her LLC, used her considerable skills as a facilitator to level the hierarchy in her LLC, a hierarchy created by her acting as both a literacy specialist, which is a supervisory position, and a group facilitator. She tried hard to build a relaxed, open community and, during observations by the research team, demonstrated a level of success. Teachers gently teased one another, shared in-the-trenches humor, and honestly questioned one another's ideas. Joanne made every effort not to be intrusive. She interrupted rarely and allowed most of the "air time" to go to the teachers. Nevertheless, there was a tendency for the teachers to look to Joanne to lead the group. Joanne recalled a time when the school's LLCs met without their "leaders" (facilitators) because the facilitators had been called away for district business. She lamented, "The work didn't get done. . . . I'm worried that there's not the commitment there, that people don't have the buy-in, that they don't see the benefit, that they don't see the real purpose" (Interview, January 2004).

Nevertheless, in their second year, the kindergarten teachers in Joanne's LLC demonstrated that they had learned to collaborate well enough to develop an action plan focused on ensuring that their kindergartners transferred what they were learning in journal writing to other writing exercises. It was clearly Joanne who led the group through the process. More than once she asked, "Okay, then, what's your plan, what's your action plan? What are you going to do within the next four weeks to try and make sure there's a difference?" And it was Joanne who repeatedly asked, "Now what kind of data are you going to bring in next time, and how will we know if we've been successful?" Although she refrained from offering answers, she was the one who posed the questions.

While the kindergarten group followed Joanne's lead, the fifth-grade team—all teachers—seemed to negotiate a "leaderless" collaboration. Over time, they began to articulate how important it was to them that they could work on their professional problems on their own. One member of Karen's group said this:

> And these meetings make a big difference because *we* say here's the problem and these are the people that are the closest to it and we've found a solution that makes the most sense in our context. So these meetings, I think, help compensate for everything else that's been pushed on us.

One of her colleagues assented, "Yeah, we make the decisions and we have the solutions!" Still another added, "I think it's empowering to be trusted to do this work." The teachers in Karen's group forged a collaborative community that collectively expanded their sense of professional responsibility and then grew in their capacity to shoulder that responsibility effectively.

The kindergarten team had certainly made strides, but they still looked to Joanne, the facilitator, to pose questions, focus their conversations, and keep them on task. While Karen's group seemed to embody a greater sense of professional autonomy and authority, Joanne's group, despite making strides in their capacity for collaborative inquiry, retained the tendency to look to supervisors for direction.

What kind of professional learning must take place in an LLC?

Constructivist theories emphasize that learning is a process of meaning making (Belenky et al. 1997; Dewey 2007; Piaget 2001; Vygotsky 1986). Successful learning, according to constructivists, demands that students exercise voice, choice, and ownership over their learning so that they can make meaning of it. They need to be able to articulate the meaning that they make, choose topics and experiences that they can connect to their lives, take ownership over what they are learning, and then apply it so it can make a difference in their lives. Moreover, according to constructivists, learning is a deeply relational activity, sparked by human interactions and nourished best in social contexts.

The rationale for the Peer Collaboration Initiative centered on creating opportunities for small groups of teachers to learn from one another and mobilize teachers to take on responsibility for improving teaching and learning in their schools. The kind of learning required for this to happen is far different from what occurs in the typical professional development session, in which direct instruction is used to deliver new strategies to a passive audience. The LLC approach, in contrast, encourages teachers to raise questions about teaching and learning, drawing on their own experiences, and to collectively pursue answers. In any collaborative group, perspectives and opinions differ, offering opportunities for teachers to question one another, challenge each other's ideas and assumptions, encourage each other to keep searching for answers, and support one another through missteps. This approach positions teachers as learners, as inquirers, as critical colleagues, and as builders of knowledge.

The kind of learning essential for teachers to think of themselves in these ways—so contrary to how sociologies of teaching describe the work and attitude of teachers—is "learning as transformation" (Mezirow and associates 2000). Most school cultures acculturate teachers to look to outside authority or to adopt traditional practices, to passively absorb and imitate ideas from outside experts, and to seek the certainty of doing what outside experts or administrators tell them to do. In too many school cultures, teachers, frustrated when some students do not respond, begin explaining away students' lack of achievement by denigrating the students themselves or their parents. Teachers in successful LLCs, however, revitalized by a common commitment to ensure student learning, challenge excuse making and question assumptions about expertise in education. Teachers in successful LLCs (like Karen's, described in this chapter as well as in chapters 1 and 3) face problems head-on; they ask what they can do about them for the sake of their students, and they begin a collective search for answers. Moreover, they question and sometimes even "unlearn" what they have known and done previously. Instead of falling back on tradition and convention when faced with dilemmas of practice, they adopt instead a "stance of inquiry" (Cochran-Smith and Lytle 1992, 1999, 2001).

Transformative learning requires a shift in attitude, from seeking certainty to continuous questioning, as well as the ability to examine assumptions or shift frames of reference. For instance, in the fall of the third year, Joanne wearily related an incident with her LLC:

> Kindergarten had their grade-level meeting last night. I was late because I had to find Yvette to talk to her. But when I went down to the kindergarten meeting, they were all four there. There are two new kindergarten teachers—new out of school and new to the building, but they have high expectations. In the grade-level meeting, we were talking about interactive read-alouds. Two of the experienced teachers were basically saying the kids aren't quite ready to listen to a story. And I thought, so there it is: low expectations.

Once the kindergarten team focused on collective inquiry, however, they stopped assuming that students were the problems and undertook lively discussions about teaching practices. In one of Joanne's LLC meetings, members of the group discussed how to "prompt" writing effectively, to help young children see the various purposes for writing, and to help them learn to recognize a graceful, "satisfying" ending to a story. Questions flew rapidly. No one appeared defensive about not having answers. Instead, they appeared comfortable with exploring various options. This, according to Joanne, amounted to a breakthrough.

That breakthrough was hard won. Joanne had worked diligently to get the group to use the cycle of inquiry process as a means to surface basic assumptions and question them. She took the group repeatedly through clarifying processes guided by such questions as: "What is the problem?" "What part of the problem do we have control over?" "What do we need to know about the problem in order to solve it?" "Is this action plan [or proposed strategy] authentically related to the problem as we see it?" As Mezirow and associates (2000) argue, transformative learning requires an awareness and a critique of "frames of reference." In Joanne's group, that meant teachers questioning their low expectations for students. Joanne credits the LLC structure for this kind of transformative learning:

It's helped me focus on being more reflective, not just with my own practice but being able to reflect with other people and to learn to help other people be able to do that. I've learned to help other people be reflective about their attitudes and practices, to question them. Questioning . . . even questioning their thinking. It's so easy to go in and tell people to do things, but probing questions and clarifying questions, they help people think about what they're doing and why. I learned about clarifying and probing questions, and then I used them in protocols, and now when I work with teachers, I think in terms of questions. To help them reflect and to come up with answers on their own, instead of me trying to solve everything.

Although the kindergarten group never took full ownership over their LLC as the fifth-grade LLC had done, the kindergarten teachers did begin to become more aware of their own assumptions and attitudes, focus their conversations, ask questions about how to do things better, and develop and implement action plans to improve student learning. Joanne explained that organizing the meetings around questions "helped me feel more comfortable being a leader in the school, whereas before I did it, but I wasn't so comfortable."

This questioning process is not always easy; it can even be downright painful. Karen told this story:

We wanted to do an approach to problem solving to improve the kids' learning. We talked about what we could do to make things better. We were always taking a simple action and coming back and talking about it and bringing the data. And it can hurt. One time I was the one sitting there, and it was someone else whose scores were significantly higher than mine on the same test. And her pre-scores weren't better than my kids. And that was hard on me. And that brought about the problem-solving approach, actually. I just decided what am I going to do about this and there was a need I had and others had and so that sparked another action plan. . . . I guess that's really the cycle of inquiry.

Karen's own struggles in her classroom and her willingness to admit mistakes lent a lot of credibility to the process. Far from being a teacher leader who was seen as a know-it-all, she, too, was a learner.

She went on to explain further. The whole group, she argued, had changed. They had moved from hiding their weaknesses to openly discussing them. She said, "What I saw was honesty, admitting you had some problems, and the ability to stop complaining and ask questions." Shifting her thoughts to her own students, she reflected:

> And then I was thinking that students also need to be honest with themselves and each other in order to move forward, and it changed every rule/every thought I ever had about running a classroom. I wanted to be their *facilitator*, not their teacher.

The "transformative learning" that Mezirow and associates (2000) have described translates into innovative action. Karen's reflections on her own transformative experiences in LLCs resulted in her using new approaches with her students. Increasingly, she used what she discovered about learning in her LLC with her own students. Thus she encouraged them to question, to share their ideas, to engage in peer critique, and to take ownership over their own learning.

Transformative learning is dialogic, akin to what Belenky and her colleagues (1997) call "connected knowing." It involves idea swapping on the basis of trusting relationships, and what Karen calls a "we're-all-in-this-together" ethos. A rapid-fire discussion about teaching writing among members of the kindergarten team illustrates what she means:

> Teacher 1: Well, we could almost do an interactive writing, where we'd all be working together.
> Teacher 2: Yes, we'd be modeling, but we'd also have child participation in with it.
> Teacher 1: So maybe we'd look at a big picture? And then discuss with the class and then do some oral work?
> Teacher 3: Oh yeah, when I'm looking at the picture, I could say, "I'm seeing such and such."
> Teacher 2: Yes, that's right, and then we could say, "Let's talk about what we think might be going on here." And then kind of develop a story line and then actually have the kids write.

Connected knowing presumes a capacity for empathy and perspective taking. Part of the charge of the LLCs is to make thinking transparent, whether it is the rationale behind a teaching practice or the facilitation of the actual LLCs. In other words, LLC processes require participants to surface their intentions and their reasons for them. This makes empathy and perspective taking less a matter of intuition on the part of the listener and more a matter of accountability on the part of the speaker. That is, the speaker develops the capacity for accounting for his or her professional decisions and actions, and the listeners learn from seeing through others' perspectives and weighing them in light of their own. An exchange between two teachers in Karen's LLC demonstrates this:

> "I'm thinking I've got to get the kids to read word problems more carefully. They just make silly mistakes. I'm going to try to give them a lot more practice."
>
> "What do you mean *silly*? Are you saying they're being careless? Are you sure practice is what they need?"
>
> "Yeah, they just rush through and don't think it through."
>
> "How would practice keep them from rushing? Are you sure they're comprehending? I mean, maybe they're really trying? Could be the reading level's too high?"
>
> "I can't believe that. The problems are really elementary."
>
> "Well, maybe the math is elementary but the reading comprehension required is higher than you think?"
>
> "Maybe."
>
> "Have you looked at the problems in terms of cultural biases? Remember that article Yvette gave us? Our kids aren't mainstream, you know. Maybe there's stuff in the questions they just don't know."
>
> "I'm going to think about that. Let me show you the problems I'm talking about."

When I visited Karen's group, I asked members about their collaboration. After a series of remarks about how good they had become at collaboration, one group member said this:

> I think my biggest fear is if they took our control away. Like, this is *our* team meeting, and we all care about it and work to figure out what the problems are and what we're going to do about them and why. Everybody's got to explain where they're coming from and make everybody else understand. You gotta tell everyone around this table there's a good reason or they're not going to buy it [laughter]. So I think that's the biggest, that could . . . that would definitely, in my personal opinion, would totally change it if someone came in and said this is what you're doing at your grade team meeting today. Um, as far as what works it's the willingness to change and to accept others' input into changing.

One of her colleagues added the following:

> Yeah, we're just listening and collaborating with other teachers
> and bouncing ideas off each other. Learning from one another
> and teachers teaching teachers. It really opens up your mind
> and it opened me up, you know, just instruction-wise what dif-
> ferent things I can do with students. And having that common
> goal and people trying to go about it differently. It really helps.
> It makes you think about different ideas. It makes you think in
> different ways.

Mezirow and associates (2000) maintain that transformative learning—
that is, learning that transforms how we think and what we do—
requires questioning the taken for granted. In these teachers' cases, they
were willing to question everyday practices with which they had been
comfortable, because they opened themselves up to questioning and to
persuasive justifications for change from their colleagues.

How should we define community within an LLC?

A statement made during a focus-group interview with Karen's group
illustrates the trusting community built by the participants:

> Everyone's, you know, very open and no one judges. And maybe
> that's what's really good. No one judges. We come in. We can
> even share [assessment] scores. We can tell how bad something
> was and no one's going to be like, "Oh, my God," and then
> look at you like you're a bad teacher. They're going to say,
> "Okay, how can we fix it? What can we do to make it better?"
> And you're not going to be judged, and no one's looking at each
> other negatively. And I like that. I come in here feeling very com-
> fortable about me, about being a teacher, even if I'm not exactly
> comfortable about what I'm doing and what the kids are doing.
> I think everyone feels comfortable with each other and what
> we're trying to do, and that's why we do so well.

An intriguing set of paradoxes is at work here. The professional learners in these groups sought comfort in one another's company, which
made them willing to discuss matters that would have made them
uncomfortable in the past. The more comfortable they grew in their
relationships with one another, the more uncomfortable they could

allow themselves to be regarding their current thinking and practices. This process opened them up to learning; it *motivated* them to learn. Interestingly, it also revealed how much they had to teach one another. In a curious way, hearing a colleague explain what she did not know put the rest of the group in touch with areas of expertise. It was, in the end, the admission of "not knowing" that made them conscious of what they *did* know, and articulating what they *did* know made them come clean about what they *did not* know. Their conversations assured them of their accumulating knowledge while whetting their appetites for further knowledge.

A community such as this one, one that fosters trust and respect, seems essential to the successful operation of LLCs. Trust and respect are not sufficient, however. In order to sustain community, participants must be able to establish common interests, serve common ends, and share common values. As the teacher says in the previous quotation, participants need to know "what we're trying to do."

Wenger (1999) describes "communities of practice" as groups of people who have interdependent relationships built around work that needs to get done. Members of such communities, he claims, come to see that they need one another to meet workplace goals. He describes these communities of practice along four dimensions: *meaning, identity, practice,* and *community.* In order to form, nourish, and sustain these communities, participants must experience their association with one another as meaningful and purposeful. They must recognize a consonance between their individual identities and the collective identity of the group so that they develop a sense of affiliation and belonging. To avoid a sense of aimlessness, these communities must focus tightly on practice, that is, workplace concerns. Finally, participants must be able to form a community that can cope with critique, disagreement, and dissent.

Wenger's insights are helpful in thinking about Joanne's and Karen's professional learning communities. Both groups established meaning and purpose through the inquiry process—articulating a question, investigating it, generating solutions, testing them out, documenting what happened, and sharing their data and experiences. In this process, they came to see themselves as learners, inquirers, collaborators, and innovators; because this sense of professional identity was not widely shared in their district, their bonds became stronger. A teacher in Karen's group said this:

> I'm different now because now I think *I'm* the one who ought
> to do something about the kids in my room, and we're all

different because we see ourselves that way and we know we
need each other because not everybody sees it like that.

The cycle of inquiry also kept the groups focused on practice, as the
LLCs' questions always emerged out of practice and oriented back to it.
Finally, Joanne and Karen had clearly demonstrated through norm-set-
ting processes the importance of monitoring and negotiating the quality
of relationships. A veteran teacher in Joanne's group said the following:

> I have to say that I wasn't too happy about some of the changes
> going on—all this assessment of kids goes against what I
> believe about early childhood education. It made me mad. So I
> kind of just checked out at first. We'd set these norms the first
> day we met, and Joanne called me on the participation one.
> And I said I didn't feel like participating in something that I
> thought was wrong. And then Joanne said we need to talk
> about this. And one of the younger teachers looked at me and
> said that the assessments were going to happen one way or
> another, and couldn't we figure out how to make it not hurt the
> kids. And then I felt bad and I thought I'd better participate.
> I've got the most experience.

While Wenger's insights are helpful, they do not go far enough. All
social contexts are permeated by issues of power (Flyvbjerg and Sampson 2001; Foucault 1980; Sarason 1991), and power has an inevitable
impact on communities. The LLCs had to contend with the power of
authority and status in a hierarchical district (see chapter 3), but they
also had to deal with more subtle forms of it, because power is not
necessarily situated atop a hierarchical pyramid. It is also dispersed
throughout social contexts, including LLCs. It is possible, therefore,
for a subordinate to wield power over a supervisor, even though the
reverse situation seems more familiar. Similarly, those at the bottom of
the pyramid exercise differing levels of power over one another. For
example, despite the fact that Joanne was a literacy specialist, she
reported in the first year after her LLC training that she facilitated a
group in which several teachers intimidated her into feeling "uncool"
because of her enthusiasm.

Hargreaves (1991) and others have warned about the dangers of
"contrived collegiality." Teachers are famously impatient with top-
down change initiatives that feel more like diversion from work than
accomplishment. Joanne and Karen struggled especially hard to convince teachers in their groups that forming a community would be a

valuable and important facet of professional work. In fact, there were times when they even had to remind themselves. Karen said this:

> And another thing I've learned about myself [is that] I can forget myself what this is about. Teachers know that my doors are open, and that's a philosophy of mine. But I put up certain barriers. Like if I'm team teaching. There are certain people I like to collaborate with and get feedback from—it's a safe place. But there are some people I really don't like collaborating with as much. I learned last week that I have to start collaborating with someone and give her more of a voice in my classroom. . . . I have to pull myself back and remember the *purpose* for collaboration—to see lots of different ways before you decide what works best.

Both Karen and Joanne learned to cement relationships in their LLCs while also making the groups productive. Both attribute their success in doing so to the emphasis on "the cycle of inquiry," wherein each group identified one or more questions that each LLC member explored both individually and collectively. Sharing a question was tantamount to creating a shared purpose. As each question was explored both individually and collectively, participants shared a common area of interest and then gained an enlarged perspective on what they could accomplish together. Having the group members fill out reflections at the end of meetings helped them reflect on the inquiry process. As one teacher explained, there was great solace in sharing questions and problems:

> Being a part of an LLC—and every teacher ought to be—is about knowing that I'm not the only one with a problem, but that everyone else is having the same thing. Knowing you're not alone and that you have to do something about it. And knowing that everyone has different strengths and different weaknesses, so I can pull on someone else's strengths in a meeting or someone can help me, you know, on my weaknesses to see if I can improve my teaching. And you know, then I can turn around and help someone else. And after awhile, we're all getting better, and so are the kids.

This quotation resonates with what Joanne and Karen would call the "true purpose" of the LLCs: internalizing responsibility for teaching and learning, sharing that responsibility in a community, recognizing problems, discussing them in a community, deciding on the next steps, taking those steps, and bringing what happens back to the community for more learning.

Collaborative relationships can be problematic, of course. Competition and egos can complicate them. In successful LLCs, however, participants cohere around the work of doing the best they can for students. They bond over work rather than depending on compatibility among personalities. As one fifth-grade teacher reported during a focus group, it was a relief to her to collaborate honestly and to give up competition among colleagues:

> We have to take away the competitiveness, too. Because if none of us . . . if we never came together to share our strengths and weaknesses, and our doors were closed, then we might think— not ill thoughts of one another—but you know we'd be much less collaborative and maybe a little more competitive. We'd be thinking, now, what's she doing and is it better than what I'm doing? And I think in this kind of work competitiveness is . . . well, it doesn't have any place when you're trying to collaborate and find answers. And when you're looking at the work and data and not who's right or wrong or something.

Karen and Joanne concur with this assessment. A focus on work and insisting on empirical data to support opinions helped defuse interpersonal conflicts. "It's always about the work and not the people," Joanne said.

One person in Karen's group offered this comment about why LLCs are important:

> I think LLCs are always going to make a positive difference in this school. Because you're around people that can help you if you need help. It's always going to make you a better person and a better teacher if you take the advice or you take all the different views. And if you're willing to change to be better at what you're doing. I don't know how it'll affect anyone outside our school as much or whether anybody will know what we're doing is important. But I know individually . . . and I think the kids will feel it.

This teacher bridges the divide between the instrumental—a strictly practical rationale for professional development—and the normative—a rationale embedded in values. Doing good work, according to her, is about being "a better person," one who is capable of taking advice, seeing other perspectives, and changing for the sake of students. Only seconds later, this same teacher added:

> I guess I don't know how LLCs could actually *hurt* someone. I guess maybe if you're not on a team that's trustworthy but, in our case, I guess I don't know how it could hurt anyone. Having a supportive community that can help you when you have difficulties, that just helps you teach better. But trust is important. And I guess I wouldn't want anyone hurt because they work in an LLC and learn to become honest.

The issue of trust is tangled in the accountability movement that affects Lincoln Elementary, as it does so many other schools. In that context, Karen reported, it is difficult for teachers to develop a sense of ownership over their own work, and issues centering on hierarchy and power have "been a part of it [the LLC initiative] from the beginning" because of Lincoln's low test scores. In the first year, she explained, she participated in a voluntary LLC with about twelve or fourteen others, "but only two were classroom teachers." The stakes were too high, she said, because of state scrutiny of test scores. The teachers who did participate were "chosen," she explained, by administrators; they were personally invited. General invitations were extended the following year, which brought more teachers into the project, and eventually, of course, LLCs were mandated and everyone participated. But by this time, the connection to LLCs and the importance of raising student achievement, as measured by test scores, had been established. The LLCs were clearly part of, as one teacher put it, "accountability to the state."

Power (1997) describes "auditing" or "rituals of verification" as a form of social control ubiquitous in Western societies. Current demands for verifying the work of teachers and schools fit into this cultural tendency. However, though Power argues that "accountability and account-giving are part of what it is to be a rational individual," he also notes, "Trust releases us from the need for checking (1)." It is, of course, a lack of trust in teachers and schools that feeds the demand for outside testing and other forms of auditing. If teachers are to account to one another for their practices, openly communicate with one another about their successes and challenges, and make their collective work both public and credible (Gutmann 1999), then they will have to build the kind of trust that allows them to air their doubts, critique their practices, admit what they do not know, and learn together. In doing so, they might learn to build public trust on their own terms.

CONCLUSION: NAVIGATING BETWEEN
SCYLLA AND CHARYBDIS

The kind of work that Joanne's and Karen's LLCs are undertaking is nothing short of culture changing, that is, moving teachers collectively from a culture of compliance to a culture of critique and possibility. Those who would keep the LLC initiative alive and thriving must gingerly navigate a course between possibility and reality.

A story from Homer's *Odyssey* serves as an apt metaphor for those who, like Joanne and Karen, enter uncharted territory. Odysseus, according to the legend, was forced to steer his ship between two monstrous forces: Scylla, who threatened to devour him and his men, and Charybdis, who threatened to drown them in her whirlpool. Joanne and Karen, facing their own unknowns, face being "eaten up" by the extra demands of working toward fundamental change, on the one hand, or being drowned by the undertow of convention and tradition, on the other. It takes great skill to negotiate a route between these two opposing forces.

The LLC initiative has the potential to solidly establish teaching as a reflective and moral practice rather than a technical one. It has the potential to aid teachers in recognizing and building practitioner knowledge. But none of this can be accomplished without investing in teachers more control, authority, and autonomy over their own work. Making collective inquiry a part of teaching practice is a particularly effective way to invest in teachers the respect and responsibility they need, and to ensure that school cultures become "learning organizations" (Senge et al. 2000). This may make some school leaders nervous, particularly in the face of escalating demands for public accountability. And it must also be said that not all teachers respond equally effectively to the kinds of demands placed on them by the LLCs.

Nevertheless, *forcing* people to act like professionals is a contradiction. Mandatory participation and taking control over the LLC agendas endanger the quality and survival of the initiative. Both courses of action undermine professional autonomy while introducing resisters into LLCs, who can then act to subvert the efforts of other participants. Asked what she thought might be the biggest barrier to the success of the LLC initiative, one fifth-grade teacher said succinctly, "I think my biggest fear is if they took our control away."

A better approach would be to heed Gutmann's call for "democratic professionalism," that is, a professionalism that incorporates both autonomy and accountability. By providing as many resources as possible to those who undertake LLC work willingly, and then by publicizing that work to the school, the district, the school board, and the larger public, school leaders could create a truly accountable school culture. In both Karen's and Joanne's LLCs, teachers have documented academic gains among their students since they began working together. Their "cycles of inquiry" have produced data, in terms of student work and improving standardized test scores, with which they can *account* for the quality of their professional labors. Those who decide not to join LLCs could be required to do a similar kind of accounting on their own terms. The aim is to negotiate a reasonable route between professional autonomy and public accountability.

The LLCs in Karen's and Joanne's district had been initially envisioned as a primary vehicle for professional development, and their principal had adopted LLCs as a way to help teachers become increasingly responsive to and responsible for students. Surrendering old models of "in-servicing" teachers, schools leaders, such as Yvette, eschew "delivery models" of instruction, not only for students but also for teachers. In other words, constructivist principles of learner-centered pedagogy ought to guide not only the learning of students but also the professional development of teachers. Constructivists honor voice, choice, and ownership as essential dimensions of learning. They believe that learners' intentions, goals, and passions *matter*. The LLCs carve out a space for teachers to express these dimensions of their work.

The healthiest and most productive learning communities have the power to make teachers, as one fifth-grade teacher put it, "feel like they can see, hear, think, and act like true professionals." They imbue teachers with a sense of professional agency and responsibility; the teachers, in turn, create communities committed to and capable of making classrooms better places for students to learn. Such communities honor the idea that everyday life in classrooms demands on-the-spot professional judgments. Learning communities, at their best, incorporate critical reading of professional literature, critical dialogue across perspectives, critical reflection on present practices, and critical inquiry into ongoing dilemmas. All of these processes provide teachers with ways of developing, honing, and exercising professional judgment so they can respond in timely and effective ways to students' evolving needs. When learning communities operate in such a manner, they have the power to break the crippling dependency on prescriptions and directives that is typical in too many schools.

Professional learning communities are not "a good" in and of themselves. They require real, protracted, demanding work. And they can go in multiple directions. Teachers can work together to build knowledge as they question their practices. They can consult outside experts and also reflect on what they have learned from experience. They can openly air their classroom struggles and ask colleagues for help. Conversely, LLC participants can concern themselves with compliance, adhere mindlessly to protocols, or devolve into resentment and passive aggression. But observing Joanne and Karen at work in their learning communities provides hope. They and others committed to LLC work are changing the culture at Lincoln Elementary. Joanne said it well:

> Probably the best thing is that the LLCs have made it acceptable to ask any questions—no matter how big or small. It's acceptable and it's *valued*. When we started talking, it may seem like a small issue, but it was important to someone else. Everyone in the group jumps in as if it were *their* problem, and they wouldn't sleep at night unless they solved it. It's the value of asking questions in our school, and it's about *caring* about those questions.

At Lincoln, the LLCs promoted authentic dialogue about real issues of practice. Teachers in Joanne's and Karen's LLCs began to think of themselves as primary agents for necessary changes in teaching and learning. They began to see themselves as responsible for and capable of ensuring students' learning. This is a tale about teachers shouldering that responsibility and building that capacity. It is the kind of story that has the power to point the way toward meaningful change in our nation's schools.

REFERENCES

Allen, D., T. Blythe, and G. Thompson-Grove. 2004. *The Facilitator's Book of Questions: Tools for Looking Together at Student and Teacher Work.* New York: Teachers College Press.

Belenky, M., B. Clincy, N. Goldberger, and J. Tarule. 1997. *Women's Ways of Knowing: The Development of Self, Voice, and Mind.* New York: HarperCollins.

Calderwood, P. 2000. *Learning Community: Finding Common Ground in Difference.* New York: Teachers College Press.

Cochran-Smith, M., and S. Lytle. 1992. *Inside/Outside: Teacher Research and Knowledge.* New York: Teachers College Press.

Cochran-Smith, M., and S. Lytle. 1999. "Relationships of Knowledge and Practice: Teacher Learning in Communities." *Review of Research in Education* 24: 249–305.

Cochran-Smith, M., and S. Lytle. 2001. "Beyond Certainty: Taking an Inquiry Stance on Practice." In *Teachers Caught in the Action*, ed. A. Lieberman and L. Miller, 45–58. New York: Teachers College Press.

Cohn, M. M., and R. B. Kottkamp. 1993. *Teachers, the Missing Voice in Education*. Albany: State University of New York Press.

Dewey, J. 1916. *Democracy and Education*. Carbondale: Southern Illinois University Press.

Dewey, J. 2004. *How We Think*. Whitefish, MT: Kessinger Publications.

Dewey, J. 2007. *The Sources of a Science of Education*. Salisbury, UK: Brunton Press.

DuFour, R., and R. Eaker. 1998. *Professional Learning Communities at Work: Best Practices for Enhancing Student Achievement*. Bloomington, IN: Solution Tree.

Elbaz, F. 1983. *Teacher Thinking: A Study of Practical Knowledge*. New York: Oxford University Press.

Flyvbjerg, B., and S. Sampson. 2001. *Making Social Science Matter: Why Social Inquiry Fails and How It Can Succeed Again*. New York: Cambridge University Press.

Foucault, M. 1980. *Power/Knowledge: Selected Interviews and Other Writings, 1972–1977*. New York: Pantheon Books.

Giroux, H. A. 1988. *Teachers as Intellectuals: Toward a Critical Pedagogy of Learning*. New York: Bergin & Garvey.

Goodlad, J. 1984. *A Place Called School*. New York: McGraw-Hill.

Grant, G., and C. E. Murray. 1999. *Teaching in America: The Slow Revolution*. Cambridge, MA: Harvard University Press.

Greene, M. 1988. *Dialectic of Freedom*. New York: Teachers College Press.

Grumet, M. R. 1988. *Bitter Milk: Women and Teaching*. Amherst: University of Massachusetts Press.

Gutmann, A. 1999. *Democratic Education*. Princeton, NJ: Princeton University Press.

Hargreaves, A. 1991. "Contrived Collegiality: The Micropolitics of Teacher Collaboration." In *The Politics of Life in Schools*, ed. J. Blasé, 46–72. New York: Sage Publications.

Hargreaves, A. 1994. *Changing Teachers, Changing Times: Teachers' Work and Culture in the Postmodern Age*. New York: Teachers College Press.

Hofmann, N. 1981. *Woman's True Profession: Voices from the History of Teaching*. New York: Feminist Press.

Lieberman, A., and D. R. Wood. 2002. *Inside the National Writing Project: Connecting Network Learning and Classroom Teaching.* New York: Teachers College Press.

Lieberman, A., and L. Miller. 1999. *Teachers Transforming Their World and Their Work.* New York: Teachers College Press.

Lortie, D. 1975. *Schoolteacher: A Sociological Study.* Chicago, IL: University of Chicago Press.

McDonald, J. P., N. Mohr, A. Dichter, and E. C. McDonald. 2003. *The Power of Protocols: An Educator's Guide to Better Practice.* New York: Teachers College Press.

McLaughlin, M. W., and J. E. Talbert. 2001. *Professional Communities and the Work of High School Teaching.* Chicago, IL: University of Chicago Press.

Mezirow, J., and associates. 2000. *Learning as Transformation: Critical Perspectives on a Theory in Progress.* San Francisco, CA: Jossey-Bass.

Piaget, J. 2001. *Psychology of Intelligence.* New York: Routledge.

Power, M. 1997. *The Audit Society: Rituals of Verification.* New York: Oxford University Press.

Sarason, S. B. 1991. *The Predictable Failure of Educational Reform.* San Francisco, CA: Jossey-Bass.

Sarason, S. B. 1996. *Revisiting the Culture of the School and the Problem of Change.* New York: Teachers College Press.

Schon, D. A. 1983. *The Reflective Practitioner.* New York: Basic Books.

Senge, P., N. Cambron-McCabe, T. Lucas, B. Smith, J. Dutton, J., and A. Kleiner. 2000. *Schools that Learn: A Fifth Discipline Fieldbook for Educators, Parents, and Everyone Who Cares about Education.* New York: Doubleday Dell.

Vygotsky, L. 1986. *Thought and Language.* Cambridge, MA: MIT Press.

Waller, W. 1967 [1932]. *The Sociology of Teaching.* New York: Wiley.

Weinbaum, A., D. Allen, and T. Blythe. 2004. *Teaching as Inquiry: Asking Hard Questions to Improve Practice and Student Achievement.* New York: Teachers College Press.

Wenger, E. 1999. *Communities of Practice: Learning, Meaning, and Identity.* Cambridge: Cambridge University Press.

Westheimer, J. 1998. *Among Schoolteachers: Community, Autonomy, and Ideology in Teachers' Work.* New York: Teachers College Press.

Wood, D. R. 2007. "Teachers' Learning Communities: Catalyst for Change or Infrastructure for the Status Quo?" *Teachers College Record* 109:3: 699–739.

7

WHAT'S TO NOT LIKE ABOUT PROFESSIONAL LEARNING COMMUNITIES?

KEN JONES

A food-loving friend of mine once said about fudge, "Sugar, chocolate, butter—what's to not like?" Likewise, we might say, about the concept of professional learning communities: collaboration, an inquiry orientation, an intention to help teachers and students learn—what's to not like? Indeed, the phrase "professional learning communities" (PLCs) has assumed an honored place in the current jargon of education, right up there with "data-based decision making," "continuous improvement," and "accountability," all presumably good things.

What is most interesting about the portrayals of professional learning communities in this book is that they dig beneath the accepted philosophies and assumptions commonly attached to the PLC concept and show some of the complex realities that accompany them. We can see good things going on, like when teachers overcome the long-standing individualistic nature of teaching to develop shared understandings and commitments with their colleagues. We can be concerned about whether teachers are being empowered or disempowered with PLCs. We can wonder about the extent of the impact on teaching and learning in the classroom. We can also ask various questions about purpose—what ends are being served by professional learning communities? In this chapter, I will explore some of these issues that the researchers in this book have raised, especially those related to the nature of teacher professionalism and how this professionalism may be constrained by current education policies and practices.

Like so much of what we do in schools, the ends of PLCs seem to be in the eye of the beholder—or maybe the practitioner or administrator or funder. For example, getting teachers together on a regular basis in the name of professional development could be a way to foster greater teacher professionalism. It could also be a means to nurture and cultivate the "common good" in our schools, whereby teachers develop consensual agreements about curriculum, instruction, assessment, climate, relationships with parents and community, or a host of other areas in order to create a healthy, stimulating, coherent learning environment for teachers and students alike. Or it could be a means, as is so often said these days, to "get everyone on board," ensuring compliance with a top-down mandate that may not be so good—for kids or for the democratic purposes of schools in our nation.

The case studies in this book provide grist for examining the realities of PLCs with respect to all of these issues. We might especially ask, as Diane Wood does in chapter 6, what being a professional means in teaching. Teacher leadership is often assumed to be an important characteristic of professionalism, but leadership for what? And who gets to decide that what? Wood asks, "Should teachers be enactors of others' expertise or critical, questioning collaborators?" This pertinent question presents the two ends of the spectrum of possibilities. We might also ask how professionalism should be defined so that it includes adherence to commonly accepted principles of quality practice, while also including respect for practitioner judgment and decision making. Where do we strike the balance so that teachers are neither fully autonomous to do whatever they want nor fully dependent on external authority for guidance and compliance? And how do we create *interdependence* among teachers in a way that honors their knowledge and experience as well as what is known about teaching and learning?

This concept of interdependence is key as we consider what teacher professionalism means. Professionals commit themselves and hold themselves accountable to certain commonly accepted standards of practice; they responsibly inquire into their own practices; and they share their understandings and practices with their peers, both informing others in their field and learning from them. At the same time, they are free to exercise their own informed judgment in being responsive to their clients. They are neither fully independent of nor fully dependent on their peers and external authorities—they are interdependent.

We see in this book a few different examples of teachers seeking such interdependence in the various configurations of PLCs. In Hillsboro, an experienced team is shown working together in a friendly and yet disciplined way, sharing each other's concerns. The teachers seem to take on responsibility for each other, demonstrating a kind of internal group accountability. They are being accountable to each other with their eyes on the well-being and learning of their students. As I see it, this is not an externally imposed accountability, defined and measured by others, but, rather, a shared sense of professional responsibility coming from within. On the other hand, Diane Yendol-Hoppey (chapter 4) describes some teachers in Florida, under a severe external state accountability system, who work fairly individualistically, but nonetheless develop important relationships with each other as they focus, understandably, on improving test scores. It is perhaps not surprising to note that the teachers in Florida had a more difficult time becoming actively engaged as a collaborative group and tended to focus on test-score data as the basis for study. External accountability, as we know it in the United States, is not known for generating teacher collegiality and self-initiated inquiry.

Debra Smith, Dick Corbett, and Bruce Wilson (chapter 5) show us what happens when PLCs are mandated and teachers operate more from a compliance mentality than from a feeling of ownership. In this case study, set in New Jersey, the authors express concern about a lack of focus on a "theory of action" related to student achievement (which usually means test scores). I understand this press for achievement, but I find myself more concerned about theories of learning and motivation in an educational era that promotes the following of directives, for both teachers and students. But I agree that participants in PLCs must have a driving sense of purpose, or they are apt to simply rely on the assumption that joint reflection will somehow lead to better teaching and learning. Can such a purpose be imposed by mandate? The authors leave that question open, suggesting that it might be a viable starting place for enabling teachers to develop their own reasons for sharing practices in a PLC. Should the purpose of PLCs be related to values associated with teacher professionalism, which engages teachers in their own inquiries into practice and standards? I sincerely hope so.

While reading these chapters, I thought about how the word "professionalism" can mean different things to different people. These days it seems that in many cases the word is used to mean working diligently to teach to state standards and to promote student success on state tests. Sometimes, though, it is used to mean resistance to that same mandated system. We see in this book that professionalism can also be about cultivating working relationships with other teachers in the building, being responsive to student needs and interests, and investigating the strengths and weaknesses of one's own practice.

As Wood points out, teacher professionalism has an inescapable subtext about power. The struggle for teacher empowerment has been a long one, whether we are talking about concerns for a living wage and reasonable working conditions, control of curriculum, or the evaluation of teaching and learning. This struggle has also been a global one: teachers around the world are often in a management/labor conflict wherein ministries, departments of education, boards of education, superintendents, and principals (usually male) set the parameters for classroom teachers (usually female). And let us not ignore the role of the world of business (again usually male) in setting the agenda for educators at all levels.

In considering power and how it conditions schooling and the meaning of professionalism, it is helpful—and important—to understand how contemporary education policies are positioned within the larger context of government power. Obviously, public schools the world over are subject to government control, but what does that mean for public school educators?

A most important factor to understand about governmental control of schools is who controls the government—and, increasingly, that control derives from the world of business and multinational corporations. Witness the increased number of "free trade" agreements that favor the movement of capital and the disempowerment of labor; the interconnectedness of government officials with business executives, including key areas of lobbying, international banking, the defense industry; and the global movement of government services toward privatization, deregulation, and the cutting back of social services. Generally called "neoliberalism," this business-oriented economic ideology has taken hold of governments around the world, often caused and enforced by U.S. military and economic power.[1]

The word "neoliberalism," though commonly used around the world, is less familiar in the United States. Often associated with the political word "neoconservatism," neoliberalism refers to the economic ideology developed most comprehensively by Milton Friedman and incorporated into what came to be known as Reaganomics. Neoliberals believe in an unrestrained marketplace and investment world, the minimization of government services (except for the military), and the turning over of public services to private ownership and management. It is the driving force behind the unprecedented disparity of wealth in the United States, which has the greatest income inequality among all developed nations and where the top 1 percent of the U.S. population owns more than the bottom 90 percent combined.[2]

We can see the current school accountability movement, as embodied in No Child Left Behind, as part of this neoliberal approach. State-defined standards are greatly influenced by the competitive needs of business and industry, with Thomas Friedman's *The World Is Flat* replacing *A Nation at Risk* with its call to fear and alarm about our public schools and the need for more "rigor." Measurements of student learning of these standards (typically through standardized test scores that act as profit/loss statements) have assumed primacy in determining the bottom-line success of schools. The testing industry, consisting of major international corporations, has assumed the major role in determining how these profit/loss statements will be constructed (making enormous profits as they do so).[3] Consistent with a capitalistic value system, ever-increasing scores (constant growth) are expected for all students. The marketplace is used as the model for "incentivizing" teachers and students with rewards and sanctions, and the option of vouchers, where public school funds are reallocated for private schools, is ever more prevalent. Learning is treated as a commodity.

The system of schooling is set up about as equitably as the capitalist system from which it springs; that is, it distinctly favors the haves over the have-nots. Predictably, the suburban privileged do well on the bottom-line testing without modifying their typically enriched curricula, while the urban and rural poor do poorly and face the downward track of skills-based curricula, regimented instruction, and less-qualified teachers. The system is, in fact, a remarkably accurate reflection of the wealth disparities created by neoliberal economics. In addition, the use of government coercion and punishment, with the rewards and punishments connected to testing, is itself reminiscent of U.S. foreign policy worldwide. Education policy in this country and in other countries throughout the world is part of a comprehensive and consistent worldview. Simply put, as critical pedagogists have long pointed out, there is a class war going on throughout the world, and education is a part of it. Governments represent business interests, which represent the wealthy. Education policies favor the wealthy and harm the poor and otherwise disenfranchised.[4]

It is an interesting aspect of this book that the cases described herein were underwritten by the Lucent Corporation; the professional learning communities are described as *Lucent* Learning Communities. I am assured that Lucent was flexible in its oversight and did not try to bring its own agenda to this project and, in fact, encouraged open exploration about the possibilities for using these groups as a means for improving teaching and learning. At the same time, I am aware of the critique about what happened to the small schools movement once the Gates Foundation got into funding small-school initiatives on a large scale.[5] The local sense of empowerment and personalization was lost, and the "fix" became one more perhaps well-meaning but ill-conceived, business-initiated external innovation meant to save schools from themselves. Various states and districts are now mandating PLCs as a required means for teacher professional development. As this book illustrates, mandating the PLC can indeed undermine its usefulness.

What does teacher professionalism mean in this context? The idea of all teachers in a school working together as a community could present a problem. Maybe the community, while laudably overcoming the long-standing isolationism of teaching, is at the same time being complicit with a nondemocratic education agenda for its students. As teachers are brought together regularly to review student work and its implications for teaching, what if the emphasis is less on adapting the system to the diverse needs of the students than it is on finding ways to change the students to meet the testing requirements of the system? And what if the culture of the particular school is indeed as I have just described in the system at large—designed to serve the haves over the have-nots? Would a teacher be acting professionally to be a collaborator, or should a professional teacher resist such collaboration?

For many, being a teacher in a public school entails making compromises and trade-offs in terms of living up to one's own ideals for education. In working with preservice teachers, I have seen the great sense of purpose and passion people bring to the profession as they enter. I have also seen what happens to novice teachers after they have been in the teaching profession for a few years. They learn to adapt to the system, making their peace with what they *must* do and figuring out what they *can* do in their own classrooms. They chafe at being treated as unskilled labor rather than as professionals. They are often frustrated and leave the profession; about one third are gone in three years, and about half are gone in five years.[6] Would a healthy system of PLCs in schools have kept some of them in the profession?

In the best of circumstances, new teachers find other like-minded teachers who have sustained their purpose and passion and have been able to work within the system to help kids learn and develop in healthy ways. I believe that thriving as a teacher in schools today, especially in those schools that serve the nonprivileged, means staying in touch with one's ideals while understanding and navigating the inequities of the system. I hear many inspiring success stories of teachers who have connected to students and made a difference in their lives. Usually these stories do not mention the students' scores on a standardized test. They depict teachers acting as professionals—using informed judgment to make decisions on behalf of their students, often despite the system. I have sometimes asked teachers to write about these experiences in my classes, and I have noticed how focusing on these stories has created a short-term community—a mini-PLC, in a way. Great power comes from the teachers as they tell their own stories rather than live up to someone else's expectations.[7]

Successful teaching is about maintaining an uplifting sense of purpose. It is about building caring relationships—this is a human enterprise, more like a family or neighborhood than like a business. Doctors who attend closely to their patients, studying unique circumstances and customizing treatment accordingly, are acting professionally. Priests and ministers who respond personally to the spiritual interests and dilemmas of their parishioners are acting professionally. Likewise, teachers who focus their attention on students and their development, as whole people, are acting professionally. Relationships might indeed serve as a powerful focus in PLCs if we are seeking to cultivate professionalism.

But there is another side to this yin-yang balancing act of being a professional. Good intentions, caring, and political perspective alone are not sufficient. Educators are focused on helping their students learn some subject matter, and not all approaches are equally effective. There is such a thing as pedagogical expertise, and a professional teacher has the responsibility to know what to do, with whom, when, and why he or she is doing it. *Informed* decision making is the key, as Wood points out in chapter 6. Professional teachers do not simply make decisions based on gut instincts. They study their students, learn about tools and techniques, look for results, question assumptions, adjust practices as necessary, and figure out what is working. Here again, however, ends matter. Are the practices being employed aimed at helping students become empowered learners? Are they designed with research in mind about how people learn, to provide varieties of opportunities for learning to all the diverse bodies, brains, and cultures in the school, to serve democratic purposes rather than authoritarian ones? Do they respect the learner? How do they serve the cause of equity?

One of the questions that this book asks us to consider, particularly toward the end of chapter 5, is whether PLCs are worthwhile if they do not bring about an increase in student achievement. What if teachers meet together and create a collaborative community, but there is no demonstrable impact on student achievement? Is this a legitimate use of teacher time? Should resources continue to be used for these meetings, or is a lack of evidence of student achievement sufficient to decide that PLCs are ineffective or unimportant?

I am of a mixed mind about this. On the one hand, I do not devalue the importance of focusing clearly and intentionally on helping students learn subject matter and grow intellectually, nor do I think teacher professional development should be simply social in nature. Professional development should help teachers be better at their jobs. As someone who teaches a mathematics methods course, I certainly think that math teachers should use their professional development time, for example, to refresh their understanding about what kinds of mathematics are more important than others in the technological age we have entered. I also hope that my students will spend time together learning to use new methods and tools and studying student work samples for formative information. The goal of such meetings would, yes, be to affect student learning—as assessed in a variety of ways.

On the other hand, however, the constant reduction of teacher development to the bottom-line evaluation about student learning is troubling and tiresome. It seems that everything in this businesslike, outcomes-based system must be justified in terms of student achievement. Would it be so bad if teachers used their time together to develop community, share ideas and practices, talk about kids, and worry about the system in which they find themselves? Must we always measure effectiveness with some sort of cost/benefit analysis, using test scores as the measure? We should value the caring and nurturing of the adults in schools as much as we do the kids. What we have done in light of our accountability mechanisms is insist on a pressurized work regimen for both adults and kids in our accountability-driven schools. The problem to fix is apparently that no one is working hard enough. There is so much to do, so much to be achieved, and so much to worry about.

In light of the fact that we should be preparing students in a democratic society to be responsible citizens, engaged learners, and intelligent analysts of information and of their own conditions, should we not open up the possibilities for what happens in learning communities? Would PLCs be less professional if teachers spent their time sharing case stories about their students, who they are, and what they are up against? Would teachers be wasting our public funds by reading and talking about the modern nature of school accountability and how the current systems of standards and testing do or do not promote democracy and equity? Would it be valuable for teachers to take time to themselves to be engaged learners by having a professional book club—reading, say, a book such as Herbert Kohl's *I Won't Learn From You—And Other Creative Maladjustments*? None of these might have a direct or measurable link to student learning, but are they not professionally appropriate?

I would argue that, yes, they are professionally appropriate. I would also argue that if the definition of professionalism were expanded to include the social and intellectual needs of the adult learners, then we would see more ownership on the part of teachers for the PLC structure, and ownership is the first step toward authentic learning. This is true for our teachers just as much as it is true for their students. Mandated PLCs with prescribed topics and outcomes have about as much chance of enhancing teacher expertise as mandated curricula with prescribed courses and assessments have of stimulating authentic student learning.[8] They may have even less of a chance, given the need for adult learners to have ownership over their own learning.

I believe that today's neoliberal zeitgeist has conditioned the way we think about work in schools, as well as in other job settings. The unrelenting emphasis is on productivity. Recently a couple of European friends mentioned to me how their cultures value the quality of life more than we do in the United States, pointing out how we are always in such a rat race, working all the time. Is this not about the constant press for profits—or, seen from the workers' point of view, the press just to make ends meet in our land of disparate wealth? In our public schools, is it not about the pressure for test scores? Recall the teacher in chapter 3 talking about feeling overwhelmed: "The tests make us feel like we have to run faster and faster, and there's so much to shore up in the kids' learning and just not enough time." Many years ago, Seymour Sarason, in his wonderfully named book *The Predictable Failure of Educational Reform*, pointed out that overwhelming teachers with too much work and too much expected change is the kiss of death for improving schools.

Another interesting theme discussed in this book centers on the use of protocols. I have used protocols in classes I teach and in a variety of professional development workshops for teachers. I find that there are always pluses and minuses in using them. Protocols focus attention and dole out time very efficiently, often giving airtime to those who might not otherwise get a word in. But they can quickly stultify a discussion, ritualizing collegial sharing in a way that takes the spontaneity and natural flow out of it. Invariably what happens in my class is that teachers only somewhat play by the rules of the protocol. They will merge times for clarifying and probing questions, either failing to see a meaningful distinction between the two types of questions or just not caring about the distinctions. The same will happen with giving "warm" and "cool" feedback—the distinctions get lost. They will sometimes talk directly to the teacher who has presented the work in an informal dialogic way rather than talking to each other about the characteristics of the work, as described in the protocol. Teachers can usually be refocused on the protocol, however, and there is often a nice friendly ebb and flow of rule following and "creative maladjustment" in my sessions.

I think this is all fine and, to some extent, even desirable. Structure is good, and so is deviation from structure. Teachers seem to like the kind of loose structure we use. I like to think of this approach not like a Robert's Rules of Order, but more informal—more like a Bob's Fairly Flexible Suggestions for Order.

But I gather from chapter 3 that the protocols were taken much more seriously in the Lucent Learning Communities, at least in Hillsboro. Here we have Lucent funding National School Reform Faculty members to come in as external consultants to show how things should be done. It feels to me a little like one of those state department "distinguished educators" who comes in to help you when your scores are bad. I would probably chafe at this kind of protocol policing, and I can imagine some teachers in this project did as well. Of course the process can be softened depending on the particular local facilitator, which I am sure also happened. The art of facilitation is important and requires that a person help keep the discussion focused while not being overly legalistic about it and bending the rules as the flow of discussion warrants. It is completely analogous in my mind to the art of orchestrating a good classroom discussion. You have a structure and a focus, and you give and take with your group in a way that honors everyone's co-creation of the exchange while still steering the ship. Overreliance on a protocol is comparable to overreliance on a textbook or curriculum. It fails to allow the ripening of the learning moment.

I learned in this book that some protocols were born from the need to capitalize on the limited amount of time in a typical teacher planning period. I should not have been surprised by this. School schedules often take precedence over learning needs. Form often does not follow function in schools, and tails tend to wag dogs in their outdated time allotments. Just as we have not found the time to do what we know is best for student learning, neither have we found the time we need for adult learning—prisoners of time, indeed, and maybe lack of imagination.

Wood raises an interesting question in chapter 3 as to whether the allotted time frames and control mechanisms of protocols prevent teachers from having meaningful self-generated opportunities for reflection and instead reinforce the role of teacher-as-technician. While this could indeed be the case in many instances, especially where the protocol is too rigidly applied or overused, I believe the tool can be used in a way that serves a useful purpose. Still, in the wrong hands, I have no doubt that protocol-governed sessions can be oppressive.

Protocol or no protocol, I have found that teachers really do need and want meaningful professional development that helps them with their jobs. As shown in this book, PLCs can provide an excellent vehicle for doing that, if they are not overly controlled by administrators. The principal in the Hillsboro case provides an excellent example of how to lead such a new initiative without taking ownership away from the teachers. As we see in that district, PLCs can be collegial, relevant, focused, ongoing, and job-embedded, and can allow choice, ownership, and opportunities for teacher leadership. Other vehicles can provide the same sorts of learning opportunities for teachers: action research, cross-school networks, discipline-based mentoring, peer coaching, and online forums and discussion groups, to name a few. The issue about effective teacher professional development is not that we do not know how to do it or that teachers are unwilling participants, it is that we have not made it a priority or funded it, and we have not allowed teachers to be in control of their own learning. In many businesses and in other professions, human resource development is carefully attended to, customized to the specific learners, and invested in. Not so much in teaching. Too often, carving out the time for teacher learning is a rear-guard action; it is hard to find the time and money. The focus is often not decided by teachers, but is more likely a "training" of some kind on how to align curriculum and instruction to the state test and the data it generates. Such practices merely cultivate teacher followership.

In many other countries, school systems provide ample time for teachers—on the clock, away from classroom duties—to pursue their own learning.[9] They have made the decision to invest the needed resources in teacher learning. We have mostly not done that in the United States. It takes a grant like the one described in this book to make it happen. Why is this? I suggest three plausible explanations.

First, and perhaps obviously, there is a women's rights issue. As Wood discusses, teaching has historically been seen as women's work and has been devalued. As evidence of this devaluation, we need look no farther than teachers' salaries and working conditions. For all the talk among educators about professionalism, the public and policy makers may not in fact view teaching as a profession. Popular perceptions of teaching include nonprofessional characterizations such as child care, unskilled labor, and part-time work (summers off and leave work at 3:30). You can hear such discussions all the time at parties. Why would someone so bright want to be a teacher? The issue goes beyond a feminist one—it often feels as if we live in an anti-intellectual society that does not value learning as much as it does, say, sports or business.

Second, there is the dominant neoliberal economic model that drives the value system and the use of public funds. Social services are on the chopping block, including education. Tax breaks are given to the wealthy and to corporations. Government spending, aside from the defense and security industries, is considered a bad thing. Money for schools or teachers is simply not a priority, regardless of rhetoric. It is no accident that our federal government is overtly hostile to teacher unions. Teacher professional organizations are a threat to a policy that is directly aimed, as I have noted earlier, at turning teachers into compliant technicians delivering a standard curriculum. All over the world, neoliberalism is antithetical to teacher unions and teacher professionalism.[10] It is not likely that our government would invest in teachers or their professional development. Teachers have been defined as the problem.

Moreover, with privatization as a key goal of neoliberal ideology, it is not just teacher professional development that is poorly funded, it is public schools themselves, especially those serving the disadvantaged. The very concept is to *not* provide adequate resources to anything related to public services. Neoliberalism is an attack on the common good in the form of deregulated private enterprise, market competition, and unrestrained capitalism. Can it be ironic or coincidental that cutbacks in school funding are happening at the very time that learning standards are ratcheted up higher and higher? I think not. These coordinated policies are intended to show that public schooling is a failed effort, and that privatization is the solution. If you have any doubts about this intention, look at what has happened to public schooling in New Orleans after Hurricane Katrina. Business interests from around the country swooped in to create a showcase for a voucher system, with full governmental support.[11]

Third, let us remember that sorting and selecting have long been the function of schools in the United States. They served this function very well with nineteenth- and twentieth-century immigrants, using a factory model, and they continue to do so in the twenty-first century. A great deal of lip service is now given to the need to educate all students to high standards, leaving no child behind, and so forth, using the language of equity. But the system simply does not work in an equitable way, and implementing a high-stakes testing system has only made it worse—we are, for example, now seeing many more dropouts than ever, especially among students of color and those who speak English as a second language.[12] Just as our neoliberal policies create huge wealth disparities in this country, their accompanying education policies create huge disparities in who is positioned to succeed in the resulting unequal society. Is there apt to be any significant investment in helping these students overcome the inequities that they have inherited—the so-called "educational debt" that Gloria Ladson-Billings talks about?[13] That would certainly be a very welcome change in direction. But such changes are not likely. Can we believe that our government will provide the time and resources needed to help schools and teachers adequately address their needs? I have not yet seen any reason to believe that will happen. The rhetoric about leaving no child behind is just that: rhetoric. The system of sorting and selecting goes on.

Finally, I would like to consider the concept of leverage that was broached at the very beginning of this book. In chapter 1, Betty Lou Whitford and Diane Wood state that learning communities are often thought to serve as "a critical leverage point for profound change." It is the work of the following chapters to unpack this idea and to explore whether it is true and under what circumstances. It is not uncommon for policy makers and corporate funders to seek that magic innovation that will, if properly done, move the mountain of public education one way or another. Whether the initiative is performance assessment, school-based decision making, cooperative learning, integrated curricula, or high-stakes testing, the hope is always that success with that effort will, in systemic fashion, cause other elements in schooling to change for the better. The idea is to somehow get a hold on this multifaceted beast we call "public school" in a way that opens the door to overall improvement. This book offers cases that belie the idea of a magic lever and instead gives us a richer, clearer picture of the complexities and contingencies of this innovation of professional learning communities. I drew a sense of hope from the cases, gathering that, for the most part, some very positive work has been generated among teachers, allowing teachers opportunities for greater interdependence and professionalism.

I was recently involved in a multiyear effort designed to align the various stages of teacher development—preservice, induction, and ongoing professional development—into a coherent whole. At the same time, there was a great deal of discussion about transforming school cultures into more collaborative environments. The lever was the creation of a school-based mentoring system for beginning teachers. The idea was to develop school councils that would attend to the training of mentors, pairing mentors and inductees, and to the overall quality of mentoring in the building, including a connection to preservice teachers in the building. Eventually, the school councils would also take on the responsibility for ongoing teacher professional development so that the entire spectrum of teacher development would be of a whole and coordinated within a school. The building would take on something of a mentoring culture, and this would create more teacher collaboration in the school. It was an ambitious vision, amply funded for five years by a number of prominent national foundations.

How did it go? Not bad. School climate surveys did show some remarkable growth in collaboration and teacher attitudes toward mentoring and professional development. This is very good news—and it is even measurable. Did the initiative cause gains in student learning? Who knows? There are too many intervening variables to be able to find out, and external standardized testing is fraught with validity challenges about making such inferences. Did it improve the working and learning conditions for adults in those buildings? By their own report, yes. And there is some indication that the system now in place will improve teacher retention. So something good has happened for teachers, but we cannot exactly say that this ambitious project leveraged systemic transformations of school culture. Mentoring is no more a magic lever than anything else. But the effort did initiate incremental change in important ways.

I see PLCs in the same vein. As this book illustrates, if done well, and not enacted for the sole (and reductionist) purpose of raising test scores, PLCs can be avenues for ongoing improvement, even though they may not be the means for larger systemic change. Teachers need to be talking to each other about their work, of that there is no doubt. Any structure that helps make that happen in a meaningful and respectful way is a plus.

We need to be mindful not to oversell the form itself, especially without consideration of the purpose it is meant to serve. Like any tool or vehicle, PLCs can be used for good or ill. Like fudge, there are varieties to like and varieties to not like. The PLCs may indeed lead to improving a school's culture, depending on the context, the people, and the time, care, attention, and investment given to it. There are many examples of teacher voices in this book that speak of success: "People are understanding each other's practice like they never have before . . . because they learn to feel safe with each other" (chapter 3); "It allows the sharing of ideas and support for common work and goals" (chapter 4); "Teachers get very excited about being able to cluster around similar concerns and really drive the conversation. Empowerment is almost magical, so invigorating" (chapter 5).

But, as we can also see in this book, PLCs can be used to make a school culture less democratic, less professional. Teachers' comments sprinkled throughout this book bear testimony to this reality as well: "Sometimes I think this LLC stuff is just another clever way to get teachers to work together in order to accomplish the district's work" (chapter 3); "The principal didn't really understand that learning communities are not committee meetings" (chapter 4); "It has turned into an obligation rather than something we wanted to do" (chapter 5).

This book is a finely detailed and honest portrayal of what is possible with professional learning communities, as well as the potential pitfalls facing PLCs. Reading it has enriched my sense of what the dimensions of a PLC are and in what directions the PLC can be taken. I feel a little like I have been allowed to observe a chameleon in its natural setting. With each different story in its different context, I saw a different color of the PLC. It is fascinating how one presumably coherent idea can take on such different aspects. One size truly never will fit all, will it?

NOTES

1. For succinct descriptions of neoliberalism, see the following Web sites: Paul Treanor, Neoliberalism: Origins, Theory, Definition: http://www.web.inter.nl.net/users/Paul.Treanor/neoliberalism.html; Anup Shah, A Primer on Neoliberalism: http://www.globalissues.org/TradeRelated/FreeTrade/Neoliberalism.asp#PoliticalversusEconomicLiberalism.

For explanations of how neoliberalism has acted as the driving force of American economic and military policies since the 1970s, see Naomi Klein, The Shock Doctrine: The Rise of Disaster Capitalism (New York: Metropolitan Books, 2007). Other illuminating works include Noam Chomsky, Failed States: The Abuse of Power and the Assault on Democracy (New York: Metropolitan Books, 2006); Michel Chossudovsky, The Globalization of Poverty and the New World Order (Montreal: Global Research, 2003); Greg Grandon, Empire's Workshop: Latin America, the United States, and the Rise of the New Imperialism (New York: Metropolitan Books, 2006); Chalmers Johnson, Nemesis: The Last Days of the American Republic (New York: Metropolitan Books, 2006). See also John Pilger's Web site: http://www.johnpilger.com/page.asp?partid=123.

For analyses of neoliberalism specific to education, see Jean Anyon, Radical Possibilities: Public Policy, Urban Education, and a New Social Movement (New York: Routledge, 2005); Henry A. Giroux, The Terror of Neoliberalism: Authoritarianism and the Eclipse of Democracy (Boulder, CO: Paradigm, 2004); Kevin Kumashiro, The Seduction of Common Sense: How the Right Has Framed the Debate on America's Schools (New York: Teachers College Press, 2008).

2. See the following for more information about the wealth disparity in the United States: David Brancaccio, "Downward Mobility—Income Disparity Overview," National Public Radio: http://www.pbs.

org/now/politics/executive2.html; David Cay Johnston, "The Income Gap Is Widening," *New York Times*, March 29, 2007: http://www.nytimes.com/2007/03/29/business/29tax.html?_r=1&oref=slogin; Huck Gutman, "Economic Inequality in the United States": http://www.commondreams.org/views02/0701-05.htm; *The Multinational Monitor*: http://www.huppi.com/kangaroo/4Inequality.htm; Jim Harney, "Financialization and Inequality": http://www.posibilidad.org/inequal.html.

3. See Barbara Miner, "Testing Companies Mine for Gold," *Rethinking Schools* 19:2 (Winter 2004/2005): http://www.pbs.org/now/politics/executive2.html.

4. See Michael Apple, *The State and Politics of Knowledge* (New York: Routledge, 2003); Paolo Freire, *Pedagogy of the Oppressed* (New York: Continuum, 1970); Henry A. Giroux, *Theory and Resistance in Education: A Pedagogy for the Opposition* (Westport, CT: Bergin & Garvey, 1988); Peter McLaren, *Critical Pedagogy and Predatory Culture: Oppositional Politics in a Postmodern Era* (New York: Routledge, 1995).

5. See Barbara Miner, "The Gates Foundation and Small Schools," *Rethinking Schools* 19:4 (Summer 2005): http://www.rethinkingschools.org/archive/19_04/gate194.shtml.

6. See Richard Ingersoll, "Teacher Turnover and Teacher Shortages: An Organizational Analysis," *AERA Journal* 38:3 (2001): 499–534; National Commission on Teaching and America's Future, *No Dream Denied* (2003): http://www.nctaf.org/documents/no-dream-denied_summary_report.pdf.

7. For a collection of case stories written by teachers focusing on the efforts to enact democratic ideals in classroom practice, see the National Network for Educational Renewal: http://www.nnerpartnerships.org/stories/index.html.

8. For a research-based analysis of the need to address student ownership in learning, see John Bransford, *How People Learn* (Washington, DC: National Academy of Sciences, 2000).

9. For international comparisons on teacher professional development, see Linda Darling-Hammond, "Teaching for High Standards: What Policymakers Need To Know and Be Able To Do" (Philadelphia: University of Pennsylvania, CPRE Publications, 1998): http://www.eric.ed.gov:80/ERICWebPortal/custom/portlets/recordDetails/detailmini.jsp?_nfpb=true&_&ERICExtSearch_SearchValue_0=ED426491&ERICExtSearch_SearchType_0=no&accno=ED426491; Forum for Education and Democracy, *Democracy at Risk: The Need for a New Federal Policy in Education* (2008): http://www.forumforeducation.org/upload_files/files/FED_ReportRevised415.pdf.

10. Mary Compton and Lois Weiner, *The Global Assault on Teaching, Teachers, and Their Unions: Stories for Resistance* (New York: Palgrave Macmillan, 2007).

11. See Bill Quigley, "New Orleans's Children Fighting for the Right to Learn," in *Truthout*, Part I (August 9): http://www.truthout.org/article/bill-quigley-part-i-new-orleanss-children-fighting-right-learn; Part II (August 10): http://www.truthout.org/article/bill-quigley-new-orleanss-children-fighting-right-learn-part-ii. Also see Leigh Dingerson, "Narrow and Unlovely," *Rethinking Schools* 21:4 (Summer 2007): http://www.rethinkingschools.org/archive/21_04/narr214.shtml.

12. See "Researchers Document High-Stakes Testing Damage, Shortcomings," *FairTest Examiner* (July 2008): http://www.fairtest.org/researchers-document-highstakes-testing-damage.

13. See "Gloria Ladson-Billings Reframes the Racial Achievement Gap": http://www.nwp.org/cs/public/print/resource/2513.

৯ 8 ৩

A LOOK TO THE FUTURE

DIANE R. WOOD AND BETTY LOU WHITFORD

Throughout this book, the authors have scrutinized learning communities in action, weighed the relative hospitality of their local contexts, and raised questions about their viability and potential. They have depicted learning communities as faltering in the face of serious obstacles and pressing demands, but they have also described scenarios in which these communities seemed to be thriving.

After chapters 1–6 were drafted, all of the authors read one another's work and came together for a half-day meeting to discuss what we had learned. We recorded, transcribed, and reviewed the conversation, which coalesced around the following questions:

1. Who should determine the work of learning communities, and what should that work be?
2. Are learning communities sustainable given the "entrenched realities" (Sarason 1996) of public schooling?
3. How can learning communities have a discernible impact on improving student learning?

Drawing on both the research reported in this book and our prior knowledge of school change, we discussed a wide range of factors bearing on these questions, but we did not fully reach consensus. For example, some participants argued that learning communities should be mandatory in order to maximize school-wide impact; others argued that voluntary participation would build teacher commitment more effectively. Some argued that teachers ought to control their groups' agendas; others said the district leadership should exert clear direction. And while all of us agreed that such groups should improve student learning, we varied in our opinions about their capacity to accomplish such a goal.

Nevertheless, there was strong agreement about one point. All of us had seen firsthand that learning communities tended to energize participating teachers and spark enthusiasm about collaborative work. Dick Corbett (coauthor of chapter 5) put it especially well. He observed that, despite obstacles and challenges,

> People still see the promise; it hasn't waned. It's not like "in the fading light of the project, people hearken back to the day when they were really excited." It's *still* there; they're excited, so *something's* going on.

Around the room, everyone nodded.

We have concluded the "something" is related to another recurring theme in this book: the professionalism of teachers. From the beginning, the project designers intended the learning communities to be a form of *professional* development, a means of facilitating "a collaborative culture within the schools, in which the school community works together to achieve mutually agreed-upon student-centered goals" (Pine and Duhl 1999, 5). And yet in many schools and districts across the United States, there is nothing *professional* about the development of teachers. In fact, they are often cast as technicians in need of retooling, especially in a high-stakes accountability context (Jones and Whitford 1997; Whitford and Jones 1998; Whitford and Jones 2000).

We contend that a professionalizing stance toward teacher learning and development is a far better course. How professional development is approached in schools ought not to position teachers as technicians, expected mainly to implement decisions made outside of the classroom. Rather, professional development should promote teachers *as professionals* by encouraging them to develop and share knowledge and exhibit agency through more clearly defined decision-making authority. In fact, we maintain that such an approach is essential if schools are to operate more equitably and attend effectively to the learning needs of all children.

In this final chapter, we first explore why fostering teachers as professionals offers the best hope for ensuring student learning. Then we summarize how learning communities can contribute to professionalizing teachers' work. Finally, we argue that, despite their promise, learning communities as we came to understand them during this research are insufficient in and of themselves as a means for professionalizing teaching cultures.

TEACHER LEARNING AND DEVELOPMENT:
A PROFESSIONALIZING STANCE

The scenarios of more successful learning communities presented in this book demonstrate that they can be fertile grounds for teacher development. Teachers in these groups socially constructed professional learning as they collectively critiqued student learning and their own practices; defined questions and problems in their work with students; engaged in reflection, dialogue, and inquiry; consulted outside expertise; and tried out new practices.

Why should schools invest in developing this kind of collaborative learning? The best of the learning communities we saw were those in which the teachers accepted the responsibility to talk honestly about the students they were failing to reach and about problems in their practice. Together they asked for advice, posed questions, and sought answers. They tried out the ideas in their classrooms and brought those experiences back to the group for continued discussion. In this way, they were taking deliberate steps to keep students from "slipping through the cracks." Such interactions have the potential to strengthen professional judgment and build greater collective capacity among teachers to respond equitably and effectively to students' learning needs.

The aforementioned, however, is not the only reason professional learning communities seem to make so much sense. The world facing our children in the years ahead will entail unimaginable changes attended by daunting challenges. Children served in public schools will need from their teachers not only the wisdom of ancestors but new dispositions and skills to meet these changes. If current students are to become adults who can play a part in shaping their world rather than simply acquiescing to conditions they inherit, then they will need the agility and flexibility of mind not only to adapt but also to negotiate, resist, assess, commit, cooperate, act, and innovate. Students need the motivation and the wherewithal to make learning a lifetime pursuit and working well with others a high priority. The dispositions we must engender in students—a lifelong thirst for learning, mental agility and flexibility, informed judgment, collaborative work, and community-mindedness—ought to be embedded in teaching cultures. Learning communities, at their best, encourage these dispositions and a renewed sense of professionalism, particularly when it comes to continuous learning, reflective practice, and enthusiastic collegiality.

That such groups have the power to foster adult learning should come as no surprise. According to many scholars of human learning, meaningful and lasting learning is most likely to take place under the following conditions (Belenky et al. 1997; Mezirow and associates 2000; National Research Council 2000):

- a socially interactive context
- opportunities to build on prior knowledge
- incorporation of learners' voices and choices
- content relevance and usefulness
- challenging opportunities for higher-order thinking, including critique and inquiry
- an ethos of continuous improvement involving peer critique, reflection, and ongoing learning

This approach to teacher learning and development is consistent with the recommendations from the National Research Council (2000) in its book *How People Learn*. According to the council, learning experiences for both K–12 students and teachers ought to be *learner centered, subject centered, assessment centered,* and *community centered*. Professional learning communities embody—or have the potential to embody—these four principles.

First, the more successful learning communities, such as those depicted in chapters 1, 3, and 6, are indeed learner centered in that participating teachers take an active role in their own learning. Moreover, these groups cast teachers in the role of professional agents rather than skilled, even efficacious, technicians. In making this observation, we propose a significant distinction between efficacy and agency. While efficacy connotes belief in one's ability to act effectively to fulfill objectives, it does not necessarily stipulate the source of the objectives. Thus it is possible for teachers to be quite efficacious in fulfilling objectives set by others. Agency, on the other hand, signifies the capacity to act on one's own intentions, even overcoming constraining cultural forces to do so.

In the best of the learning communities, we observed a growing sense of agency as participants developed confidence about establishing and pursuing their own mission-related objectives, even when those objectives ran counter to a prescribed curriculum. Put differently, they felt a keener responsibility to attend to students' individual needs than to comply with directives. This kind of agency—acting in the best interests of the client—is a trademark of professional practice. Coincidentally, it is also a necessary attribute of the lifelong learner because, as the National Research Council explains, voice and choice matter a great deal in all human learning, including the learning of teachers.

Second, chapters 3, 4, and 6 demonstrate that learning communities can provide a subject-centered environment for teacher learning. These

chapters contain examples of teachers reading and discussing professional literature and searching for answers to their dilemmas and problems. The descriptions and scenarios of the best learning communities
suggest that they foster habits of reflection, critique, and inquiry; motivate teachers to confront their doubts and questions; and then facilitate
the pursuit and construction of new knowledge. This involves both
looking to outside expertise and analyzing lived classroom experiences.

According to Cochran-Smith and Lytle (1999), this is the process of
building much-needed "knowledge *of* practice." They argue that
"knowledge of practice" brings together outside knowledge or "knowledge *for* practice" and practitioner knowledge or "knowledge *in* practice" for the purposes of interpreting classroom processes, raising
questions about them, pursuing lines of inquiry, and constructing new
knowledge. As they put it:

> The third conception of teacher learning involves what we call
> "knowledge of practice." Unlike the first two, this third con-
> ception cannot be understood in terms of a universe of knowl-
> edge that divides formal knowledge, on the one hand, from
> practical knowledge, on the other. Rather, it is assumed that the
> knowledge teachers need to teach well is generated when teach-
> ers treat their own classrooms and schools as sites for inten-
> tional investigation at the same time that they treat the
> knowledge and theory produced by others as generative mate-
> rial for interrogation and interpretation. In this sense, teachers
> learn when they generate local knowledge *of* practice by work-
> ing within the contexts of inquiry communities to theorize and
> construct their work and to connect it to larger social, cultural,
> and political issues. (250, emphasis in original)

Several chapters in this book reveal teachers doing precisely what
Cochran-Smith and Lytle describe.

Third, the learning communities we studied were generally assessment centered. Sometimes this meant that their deliberations focused
narrowly on standardized test scores, as was the case in some learning
communities in all project sites. Occasionally the teachers themselves,
anxious about test scores, steered their learning communities in that
direction; other times building, district, or state administrators declared
raising test scores the primary function for the groups.

There were, however, examples of learning communities that adopted
a far different approach to assessment-centeredness. Although such communities accepted test scores as one fund of data, they developed an

extended notion of what ought to count in assessing their work. For instance, they monitored the quality of their deliberations by weighing the degree to which they adhered to norms they established for their work. They also attended to the impact on student learning by trying out new strategies and systematically observing and assessing student work and behavior. In the most promising learning communities, the teachers developed an array of new professional dispositions, including an appetite for critical self-assessment, a capacity to name and internalize high expectations for themselves and students, and a desire to ask and then determine how well they were doing in fostering their own and student learning (see chapter 6 especially).

Finally, the National Research Council claims that learning experiences ought to be community centered. Of course, simply dubbing a group a "learning community" does not necessarily mean that the group is community centered. Being community centered requires that groups catalyze professional bonds around shared commitments to students, and that they invigorate collective efforts to improve student learning.

As Diane Yendol-Hoppey points out in chapter 4, some groups called "learning communities" are really ordinary committees. While the latter may have delegated power to make decisions, the former not only make decisions but do so as a result of dialogue, reflection, and inquiry. In most circumstances, a larger authorizing body forms committees and charges them with specific roles and responsibilities. Learning communities tend to evolve their own purposes, roles, and responsibilities. Successful learning communities of teachers, though they also may be formed by administrative authority, can take quite unpredictable pathways, because their deliberations tend to be iterative and meandering. Thus learning communities are far more likely to develop organically than committees and far more difficult to control from the outside. Authentic communities tend to develop when people establish shared purposes and recognize how they can accomplish those purposes together. Authentic communities tend to last when they have the room and the authority to adapt and innovate as original purposes are fulfilled and new ones develop.

CAN LEARNING COMMUNITIES ADVANCE A PROFESSIONALIZING STANCE?

What have we learned about how learning communities contribute to a professionalizing stance toward teacher learning and development?

During our research, we were able to distinguish different types of groups by the influence they had and thus the potential impact they could have on how teacher learning and development are viewed and supported.

Some groups likely had little or no impact. These might have been learning communities that did not stay together long enough to gel as a group. They may have met too infrequently or not long enough during any one session. The group's coach may not have been skilled enough to provide needed guidance, or the group members may have experienced a mismatch between the issue someone brought to the group and the protocol selected to guide the deliberations. Group members may have perceived their task as practicing as many protocols as possible, learning to do each step well before they could dare tackle the more important issues of teaching and learning. They may have devoted much of their time to ice breakers and trust building, only to see their group reconfigured the next year. Or, group members may have intentionally avoided sharing artifacts of students' learning or their own teaching because it was more comfortable simply talking about a professional dilemma using the very popular "consultancy protocol," obtaining feedback they could choose to use or not at their discretion, rather than collectively examining evidence bearing on teaching and learning. In these situations, any change in classroom behaviors would be up to the individual teacher. Even during the national coaches' trainings during the first two years of the initiative, NSRF facilitators found it challenging to get the novice coaches in their sessions to contribute samples of student work.

In all of these situations, there would be little in the life of the group that would disrupt the norms and ways of being that the group members brought with them into the learning community. Such groups would not be equipped to serve as vehicles for change. Worse, they could be used as evidence for why learning communities "won't work."

With other groups, teachers thought of themselves differently and behaved differently as a result of their participation. Their sense of responsibility expanded beyond their own classrooms to their colleagues' classrooms. They no longer threw up their hands or played the blame game when faced with struggling students but reached out to colleagues for help and redoubled their efforts to reach even the most challenging students. They read professional literature, collected data as they innovated, made their teaching public, and invited critique.

These are important gains, but there are core questions to consider: To what end are learning communities directed? Should they be a means of improving teaching and learning within the present organizational context of schools? Should they coexist within the current hierarchical power structure of schools, or should learning communities become part of a larger effort to transform the system? Can they contribute to advancing a professionalizing stance toward teacher learning and development? We argue for the latter, especially given a series of events that occurred in the Hillsboro District toward the end of our study.

As described in chapters 3 and 6, Joanne, Karen, and the teachers in their learning communities adopted profoundly different professional identities as a result of their LLC participation. Their ideas about what they could and ought to be doing for struggling students changed, as did how they should hold themselves and one another accountable. At the root of these changes was an empowering vision of what teachers could do together to make student learning more inclusive and equitable and their own work more professional and public—at least within their LLCs. For some, the habits of mind and practice originally incubated in the LLCs generalized to other settings (see Joanne and Karen in chapter 6).

Despite these gains, a deflating incident occurred. During the summer, after the kindergarten and fifth-grade teams had made real progress in solidifying their community and even saw gains in test scores, a stack of boxes was delivered—unannounced—to the school. The boxes were full of basal readers. The new superintendent had ordered them and mandated their use. The principal groaned:

> Sheesh, we've worked so hard to get teachers to use an eclectic approach and develop a repertoire of strategies. I thought we were on a roll. And then the basals arrive!!! We're just going to have to figure out how to use them as resources and not as the whole curriculum. . . . I can't work with teachers as professionals if we are all just going to be told what to do.

Joanne and Karen concurred, with the latter explaining:

> We've finally gotten to the point we see ourselves and each other as decision makers. We're finally seeing we can really achieve something together, do better by the kids, and then this happens!

This episode underscores Sarason's (1991) point that school change is laden with power issues. By mandating basal readers for teachers, the new superintendent threatened to undermine learning community work that had been embraced by a substantial number of Lincoln Elementary's teachers. Moreover, the mandate was a stark reminder of teachers' ultimate powerlessness as decision makers about policy.

While the Lucent-funded Peer Collaboration Initiative had a lofty, an ambitious, and even a transformational goal aimed at significantly altering the professional cultures of schools, so too are many educators and educational researchers working toward the not-yet-achieved goal of creating the conditions under which the learning of all children is ensured. Part of the difficulty in directing resources to this goal is that we have yet to believe that teachers are up to the task. We demonstrate this lack of trust time and again by asking them to teach so that every student reaches an array of standards across multiple disciplines, and then we impose one reform strategy after another, increasing the demands, the stakes, and the responsibility—but not the authority. We are willing to leave our children in their care for six or seven hours a day, but we have yet to base improvement strategies on the confident belief that, given the right conditions, teachers can ensure the learning of all children and then go about creating those conditions.[1]

As a consequence, many change strategies are designed to operate within the existing system of the educational organization—a hierarchical, often paternalistic, or even infantilizing distribution of power and authority. Most of our change strategies are attempted without making significant changes in this system. The results, at best, are marginal improvements.

Table 8.1 captures two sets of conditions. One set (System Enhancement) characterizes the "improve the current system" mentality, which in this era of high-stakes accountability typically means enhancing the "teacher-as-technician" view of professional development. The other set of conditions (System Transformation) proposes what we would characterize as a "teacher-as-professional" stance toward professional development.

Our argument is focused on the potential effectiveness resulting from supporting a professionalizing stance toward teacher learning and development. In the context of other discussions of the need to professionalize teaching as an occupation, our argument rests primarily on empowering teachers as professional agents as a necessary condition to ensuring the learning of all children. As such, it narrows the focus to learning and the invention of on-the-ground strategies rather than an expectation that teachers will primarily implement solutions that have been developed elsewhere.

Table 8.1 lays out starkly different views of what learning communities ought to be and what the professional role of teachers ought to be. In the right-hand column, teacher work becomes not only public but also grounds for constructing knowledge. Teacher collaboration, rather

Table 8.1. *Learning Communities: Enhancement or Transformation?*

	System Enhancement	*System Transformation*
Teacher Work	Make more public, open to peer critique and easily monitored; conform to "best practices"	Make more public, open to peer critique; use as grounds for theorizing and constructing knowledge
Role of Collaboration	"Get everyone on board" to fulfill predetermined state, district, or school objectives; elicit everyone's best thinking to that end	Promote authentic collaboration around shared questions and goals; engage teachers in constructing goals, ends, and processes; create new solutions and new innovations regarding student learning
Degree of Autonomy	Encourage critique and inventiveness within confines of hierarchically determined institutional purposes and directives	Encourage professional autonomy within confines of a shared mission, collectively established goals, and collectively vetted promising practices
Professional Competence	Indicated by mastery of best practices, ability to work with colleagues, grasp of system goals and priorities	Indicated by inquiry stance, capacity to respond to ever changing student needs, commitment to collectively established mission
Knowledge/Expertise	"Knowledge for practice" sought from outside sources; "knowledge in practice" shared in order to improve system-approved practices and fulfill system established objectives	"Knowledge of practice" constructed through continuous and systematic inquiry, critique, and assessment of classroom practices, coupled with search for relevant outside knowledge
Professional Accountability	Situated in individuals and dependent on administrative oversight, compliance with system's goals and objectives and system-established measures of student achievement; indicated by practices conforming to system priorities	Situated in professional community and internalized sense of responsibility; dependent on peer critique and self-monitoring as well as outside assessments; indicated by inventive and effective responses to students' learning needs as assessed by multiple measures; indicated by practices consistent with shared mission

than simply fostering cooperation and compliance, encourages collective inquiry and creative imagination. Teacher autonomy is restricted not by administrative will but by the demands of school missions, shared goals, high expectations, and research-based, collectively critiqued practices. The ideal of a competent teacher shifts from someone who masters skills and job descriptions to someone who can effectively respond to all students' needs, work creatively with colleagues, and commit to shared professional goals. Professional knowledge is no longer seen as something coming from outside of the profession but as multidimensional and includes teachers playing a part in its construction. Finally, teacher accountability is not solely located in individual professionals but also in professional communities as teachers internalize shared commitments, subject their work to peer critique, account to one another for their decisions and practices, collect and pay attention to a wide variety of student data (including student work), and monitor themselves as they strive to respond to ever-changing student needs. Overall, they are agents in a profession for which they have a sense of shared ownership.

CONCLUSION

As we have thought and written about professional learning communities, we have been forced to reflect on our own values. It has been helpful to consider Heifetz's (1998) notion that "Rigor in social science does not require that we ignore values; it simply requires being explicit about the values we study" (14). Heifetz developed his thinking about social science because of his studies of leadership, which he believed could not be conducted in a value-neutral manner. We believe his point is also applicable to the study of professional learning communities, because, at their best, they imbue leadership qualities in teachers. Heifetz's stated values about leadership resonate with Gutmann (1999) when she calls for leadership "suitable to a democracy" (8), that is, leadership that fosters and inscribes democratic ideals and practices and allows for leadership to develop at all institutional levels. Moreover, Heifetz's thinking would have been praised by Dewey (1954), who warned about "an eclipse of the public" resulting from bureaucratic, sometimes authoritarian, workplaces and institutions. Dewey warned that such systems promote disengagement and discourage participation. If teacher learning communities are to reach their full potential, then school administrators will need to welcome and nurture authentic and strong teacher leadership.

Public schooling, after all, is another human enterprise that cannot be adequately described or analyzed in value-neutral terms, nor can it be decoupled from the common good. Schools in this society were established to serve a democratic public, and they were inspired by particular notions about human rights and responsibilities. Thomas Jefferson, Horace Mann, Booker T. Washington, W. E. B. Dubois, Mary McLeod Bethune, John Dewey, and many other luminaries of public education have argued eloquently for generations that public schooling is essential to a participatory and democratic public, to self-governance, and to a fair and just society. Nevertheless, as Ken Jones persuasively argues in chapter 7, our public schools could be and should be serving our democracy better. They could be and should be educating students more equitably and compassionately. And they could be and should be generating school cultures that foster practices in and appreciation of democratic life.

Although we realize they are rare, we have described a few learning communities that gesture toward more creative possibilities for the teaching profession. In these groups, teachers raised their voices and established common interests and goals for the sake of student learning. The teachers in these communities were acting not out of a concern for compliance but out of a commitment to a shared mission—improving *all* students' learning. As they pursued that mission, they discovered the power of social practices necessary for participatory democratic processes. They established communities that contained dissent as well as agreement, critique as well as support, resistance as well as cooperation, and conflict as well as compromise. Indeed, they created communities that became microcosms of democratic relationships working toward the common good.

If schools are going to serve the nation's children more equitably by preparing *all* of them to successfully handle the unknowns of the future, groom them for participation in a democracy, and equip them to contribute to an increasingly endangered "small blue planet," then teachers themselves will need to be continuous learners, reflective practitioners, and enthusiastic colleagues. Professional learning communities, if they are allowed to be indeed *professional,* are a promising means for helping that vision become a reality.

NOTE

1. See, for example, *Measuring What Matters: The Effects of National Board Certification on Advancing 21st Century Teaching and*

Learning, Center for Teaching Quality, 2008, retrieved at http://www. teachingquality.org/pdfs/TS_NB_report0708.PDF.

REFERENCES

Belenky, M., B. Clincy, N. Goldberger, and J. Tarule. 1997. *Women's Ways of Knowing: The Development of Self, Voice, and Mind.* New York: HarperCollins.

Cochran-Smith, M., and S. Lytle. 1999. "Relationships of Knowledge and Practice: Teacher Learning in Communities. *Review of Research in Education* 24: 249–305.

Dewey, J. 1954. *The Public and Its Problems.* Athens, OH: Swallow Press Books.

Gutmann, A. 1999. *Democratic Education.* Princeton, NJ: Princeton University Press.

Heifetz, R. 1998. *Leadership without Easy Answers.* Cambridge, MA: Harvard University Press.

Jones, K., and B. L. Whitford. 1997. "Kentucky's Conflicting Reform Principles: High-Stakes School Accountability and Student Performance Assessment." *Phi Delta Kappan* (December, 1997): 79:4: 276–81.

Mezirow, J., and associates. 2000. *Learning as Transformation: Critical Perspectives on a Theory in Progress.* San Francisco, CA: Jossey-Bass.

National Research Council. 2000. *How People Learn: Brain, Mind, Experience, and School: Expanded Edition.* Washington, DC: National Academies Press.

Pine, L., and J. Duhl. 1999. "Proposal to the Lucent Technologies Foundation from the Philanthropic Initiative." Unpublished manuscript.

Sarason, S. 1996. *Revisiting "The Culture of the School and the Problem of School Change."* New York: Teachers College Press.

Whitford, B. L., and K. Jones. 1998. "Assessment and Accountability in Kentucky: How High Stakes Affect Teaching and Learning." In *International Handbook of Educational Change.* ed. A. Hargreaves, A. Lieberman, M. Fullan, and D. Hopkins, 1163–78. Dordrecht, the Netherlands: Kluwer Academic Publishers.

Whitford, B. L., and K. Jones, eds. 2000. *Accountability, Assessment, and Teacher Commitment: Lessons from Kentucky's Reform Efforts.* Albany: State University of New York Press.

ABOUT THE AUTHORS

DICK CORBETT is an independent educational researcher who spends his time studying school reform, primarily in low-income settings. Recent projects include examining efforts funded by the Benwood, NEA, Osborne, Lyndhurst, and Public Education Foundations to raise student achievement at all levels of the Hamilton County, Tennessee school system; the implementation of collaborative learning communities in two New Jersey districts; the effects of the Commonwealth Institute for Parent Leadership's training program on parents' subsequent involvement in Kentucky schools; and a Michigan Middle Start pilot initiative to improve math instruction in rural Michigan schools. Past work has entailed investigating several Comprehensive School Reform models, including Middle Start, Onward to Excellence II, Talent Development, Different Ways of Knowing, and the Mississippi Arts Commission's Whole Schools Initiative. His three most recently published books are *Creating and Sustaining Arts-Based Reform: The A+ Program*, coauthored with George Noblit, Monica McKinney, and Bruce Wilson (Routledge, 2008), *Effort and Excellence in Urban Classrooms: Expecting—and Getting—Success with All Students*, coauthored with Bruce Wilson and Belinda Williams (Teachers College Press, 2002), and *Listening to Urban Kids: School Reform and the Teachers They Want* (State University of New York Press, 2001), coauthored with Bruce Wilson.Corbett received his PhD in education from the University of North Carolina-Chapel Hill.

KEN JONES is an associate professor and the director of teacher education at the University of Southern Maine. His interests include classroom assessment, mathematics education, case story development, and policy analysis related to school accountability. He has been a middle

181

school teacher, a district mathematics specialist, and the director of a school-university partnership for teacher professional development. He recently edited *Democratic School Accountability: A School Improvement Model* (2006, Rowman & Littlefield).

DEBRA R. SMITH is director of the Program Evaluation and Research Group at Lesley University. Her experience in education over three decades includes teaching in a variety of settings, from preschool to graduate school; program, curriculum, and assessment design; and research and evaluation. She was the founding director of the Collaborative Inquiry and Development Group at the University of Southern Maine, where she served as a principal investigator for several projects funded by the Lucent Technologies Foundation. Her work over the last several years has focused on teachers' deepening understanding of students' learning through assessment and collaborative inquiry. She holds a PhD from Lesley College.

BETTY LOU WHITFORD is dean of the College of Education and Human Development and professor of education at the University of Southern Maine. She has published widely in the areas of school reform and teacher education, including contributions to yearbooks and peer-refereed journals. She taught high school social studies in Virginia Beach, Virginia, and has held academic and research positions at Teachers College, Columbia University; the University of Louisville; and the University of North Carolina at Chapel Hill, where she earned her AB, MAT, and PhD degrees. With Ken Jones, she coedited *Accountability, Assessment and Teacher Commitment: Lessons from Kentucky's Reform Efforts* (2000, State University of New York Press), and with H. Dickson Corbett she coedited the SUNY series on Restructuring and School Change.

BRUCE L. WILSON is an independent researcher. He also has served as an adjunct faculty member at Teachers College, Columbia University. He is currently engaged in several longitudinal research and evaluation projects, all of which focus on improving teaching and learning conditions in schools with populations of high poverty. With support from government agencies, private foundations, and universities, the primary goal of this work is to produce information that will be helpful to schools and agencies helping schools as they refine the work they are doing to improve learning for all students. This research has been published in a wide range of scholarly journals and books. His two most recent books are *Effort and Excellence in Urban Classrooms: Expect-*

ing—and Getting—Success with All Students, coauthored with H. Dickson Corbett and Belinda Williams (Teachers College Press, 2002), and *Listening to Urban Kids: School Reform and the Teachers They Want* (State University of New York Press, 2001), coauthored with H. Dickson Corbett. His academic training was at Stanford University, where he earned an undergraduate degree in sociology and a PhD in sociology of education.

DIANE R. WOOD, after twenty years of working in high schools as a teacher and an administrator, earned her doctorate at Teachers College, Columbia University. Currently an associate professor in Initiatives in Educational Transformation at George Mason University, she was formerly at the University of Southern Maine. She focuses her scholarship on inclusive, democratic learning communities and on narrative inquiry as a methodology for both research and professional development. She coauthored with Ann Lieberman *Inside the National Writing Project* (Teachers College Press, 2002) and coedited *Transforming Teacher Education* (Bergin & Garvey, 2001). Her articles have appeared in *Anthropology and Education Quarterly, Curriculum Theorizing, Harvard Educational Review, Educational Leadership,* and *Teachers College Record.* She has given numerous presentations at national conferences. In 2000 she was awarded a joint residency at the Rockefeller Center in Bellagio, Italy.

DIANE YENDOL-HOPPEY is the director of the Benedum Collaborative and professor of education at West Virginia University. She spent the first thirteen years of her career in education, teaching in Pennsylvania and Maryland. In her work at Pennsylvania State University, the University of Florida, and now West Virginia University, she has focused on job-embedded teacher professional development and the cultivation of teacher leadership. Her research explores how powerful vehicles for teacher professional development, including teacher inquiry, professional learning communities, and coaching/mentoring, can support school improvement. She has authored numerous studies that have appeared in such journals as *Teachers College Record* and *Journal of Teacher Education.* She is the coauthor (with Nancy Fichtman Dana) of two books, *The Reflective Educator's Guide to Classroom Research* (Corwin Press, 2008) and *The Reflective Educator's Guide to Mentoring* (Corwin Press, 2006).

INDEX

Note: Page numbers in *italics* indicate figures; those with a *t* indicate tables.

Abbott districts, 95–96, 105
accountability, 17, 28, 62–65, 73–91, 143, 145
  interdependence and, 151
  system enhancement for, 175–77, 176t
Achinstein, B., 50
action plans, 8, 123–24
action research, 34, 112–15, 159
agency, 60–61, 67, 145, 169, 170
  See also empowerment; professionalism
Alcatel corporation, xi, 93
American Educational Research Association, 34
"America's Choice" reform model, 97t
Anyon, Jean, 163n1
A-Plus Acccountability Program, 73
Apple, Michael, 164n4
apprentice coaches, 30, 45, 94, 103–4, 111
Asher, Carla, 37n1
ATLAS protocol, 11, 16–17, 29
autonomy, xiii, 56–57, 60–61, 74, 126–27, 130, 176t, 177
  See also empowerment

Backiel, Chris, 38n1
Beach County Public School System, 74–91
  See also Florida school system
Bedder, Ken, 38n1
Belenky, M., 136
Bethune, Mary McLeod, 178
Brabham, E. G., 87
Brancaccio, David, 163n2
Bransford, John, 164n8
Buchovecky, Eric, 19n3

capacity building, 45
Center for Teaching Quality, 179n1
change. *See* transformation
Chomsky, Noam, 163n1
Chong, Ji-Sung, 38n1
Chossudovsky, Michel, 163n1
Clayton, Christine, 38n1
coaches, 7–8, 27
  apprentice, 30, 45, 94, 103–4, 111
  challenges of, 85–86
  external, 25, 29, 45
  peer, 159
  support for, 29, 36
  training of, 22–24, 30, 36, 44–47
  See also facilitators
Coalition of Essential Schools (CES), 76
Cochran-Smith, M., 83, 171

185